M000040582

VITAL

A TORCH FOR YOUR SOCIAL JUSTICE JOURNEY

Be Brave!

VITAL

A Torch For Your Social Justice Journey

By
Kyle C. Ashlee and
Aeriel A. Ashlee

Brave Space Publishing
Cincinnati, Ohio

VITAL: A Torch For Your Social Justice Journey © 2015 by
Kyle C. Ashlee and Aeriel A. Ashlee

All rights reserved. Copyright under Berne Copyright
Convention, Universal Copyright Convention, and Pan-
American Copyright Convention. No part of this book may be
reproduced, stored in a retrieval system, or transmitted in any
form, or by any means, electronic, mechanical, photocopying,
recording or otherwise, without prior permission of the author.

ISBN: 978-0692532980

Printed in the United States

Cover Design by Khushal Chand Khatri
Interior Design by Sheenah Freitas

To order, visit www.ashleeconsulting.com
Reseller discounts available.

TABLE OF CONTENTS

INTRODUCTION

Do your little bit of good where you are.
— Desmond Tutu

You're at a baseball game. You're high above the field and have a great view. You can see all the players shuffling around the bases. The weather is just right, you've got a cold drink in your hand, and all is well in your world. As you look around the stadium you notice three fans standing just behind the fence at the edge of the field. They are of varying heights and this significantly impacts their ability to see the game.

The tallest of the three towers over the fence and can see the whole field without a problem.

The fan of middle height can barely see over the fence if she stands on her tippy toes. She's exhausted from the effort, but every now and then she's able to get a glimpse of the game and that gives her enough hope to keep trying.

The shortest fan doesn't have a chance. No matter how hard he tries to climb or jump up the fence he can't see over the top. When he looks to the fan of middle height for a boost she's too tired to help. And the tallest fan is too engrossed in his enjoyment of the game to notice how the others are struggling.

You've been observing now for five minutes, and the scene continues to bother you. *This is so unfair,* you think to yourself. *Just because one fan is taller than the others doesn't mean he deserves a better view of the game. He didn't earn it or otherwise do anything to get that view. Why do the others have to work so hard to get a glimpse of the action?*

"The world is so unfair. I wish there were more equality," your friend says. A few moments ago, he had noticed how your eyes were fixated on the scene and he's been watching it ever since.

"Yes!" you respond. "Equality now!"

As if prompted by your exclamation, you notice a man is now carrying three equal-sized boxes for each fan to stand on so that they can get a better view of the game. Your heart bursts with pride because each fan was treated with equality. In unison, all three fans step up onto their box and now your heart sinks. The tallest fan stands high above the fence and now has an even greater view. The fan of middle height can now see the game without straining. The shortest fan is still unable to see the game.

"At least someone tried to help," your friend says.

"True. But I think the shortest fan should get an extra box," you respond.

"But that wouldn't be fair then, would it?" your friend asks.

"But it wasn't fair to begin with," you say.

This is where social justice thrives. Instead of equality, social justice aims to provide resources and opportunities that are specific to each person's situation. Rather than seeking equality, a blanket approach that can be applied across the board, social justice strives for equity as the larger outcome that can arise when actions are tailored based on individual circumstances.

Many people use the term equality as the ultimate aim for social justice. While equal treatment is a nice idea, it doesn't actually result in fairness. Instead, the idea of *equity* seems to align much closer with the goals of social justice: assessing each individual's specific needs and contexts before determining a course of action.

A social justice lens allows us to more accurately assess the needs of each fan. For example, it's obvious that the tallest fan doesn't need a box to comfortably watch the game. The fan of middle height, however, could use some resources and so should be provided one box to make sure she can see the game. Lastly, the shortest fan should get two boxes to properly see the action.

This scenario is the way privilege and oppression play out in our society. Many of us want to do something, and we embrace equality because it feels like the natural antidote to injustice. But the world's inequalities run deep and demand deeper solutions.

Our fifteen years of experience, study, and travel have led us to believe that it will take all of us to commit to a social justice journey if we want to address and resolve existing social inequities. If you're still reading, it's likely you're either looking to begin your journey or have been journeying for years.

Welcome! May our VITAL practice be the torch that helps light your way.

—KYLE & AERIEL ASHLEE

CHAPTER 1:
WHAT IS SOCIAL
JUSTICE?

Never forget that justice is what love looks like in public.
—Cornel West

The term "social justice," like many ideas in our country, has unfortunately been warped and split along political lines. On one side it's viewed almost as a profanity; a concept that represents taking resources from those who earned them and delivering them to those who didn't. On the other side it's often viewed as a concept for all things related to peace and love rather than as an ideology with immense practical application.

In reality, however, social justice is none of the above. In their seminal book, *Teaching for Diversity and Social Justice*, authors Maurianne Adams, Lee Anne Bell, and Pat Griffin define social justice as, ". . . full and equal participation of all groups in a society that is mutually shaped to meet their needs. Social justice includes a vision of society that is equitable and all members are physically and psychologically safe and secure."

While this might seem like a utopian and idealistic picture of the world, the process implied is actually quite complex. Social justice involves a continual process of developing awareness, communicating lived experiences, negotiating different needs, and broadening the process of decision-making to include all voices. In other words, the process of social justice is just as important as the end goal.

For those who don't often think about the ways in which our society unfairly treats people because of matters like race and gender, the idea of social justice might seem daunting. Sure, many can agree that concepts like racism and homophobia are wrong, but actually talking about these issues can be uncomfortable. Understandably, many take the approach of trying their best to treat everyone fairly and then assuming this is enough to do their part in supporting equality for all.

But for those who value social justice—those who strive to live it—the story could not be more different.

In *The Matrix*, a 1999 sci-fi action film starring Keanu Reeves and Laurence Fishburne, the character Neo (played by Reeves) has a choice: he can take the blue pill and go on believing whatever he wants to believe, or he can take the red pill and see the "true nature" of the world around him.

Similarly, people who work toward social justice have taken the red pill and their entire world looks different as a result. Once having been exposed to the realities of structural oppression, the social justice journeyer starts to see injustice all around them. They see it in the words we use and the stories we tell. They see it in the movies we watch and the books we read. They even see it in the subtle messages children are taught through toys, games, and media.

Many who are passionate about social justice often feel like they are living in a different reality than the rest of society. While others go about their lives under the influence of the blue pill, the social justice journeyer understands that the only way to change things for the better is to first be aware of the problems that need to be addressed. They also understand that trying their best to treat everyone fairly is only the tip of the iceberg. The social justice journeyer believes that ending oppression requires fundamental change on the personal and societal levels. They also understand the words of Martin Luther King, Jr. when he said that personal freedom is inherently connected to the freedom of others, and that no one is free if others are oppressed.

Are you ready to embark on a social justice journey? If you've already taken the red pill you know how tremendously difficult, yet fulfilling, a life committed to social justice can be. For you, there's no going back.

Even the most committed social justice journeyers however, require inspiration. Just as the light of a torch guides the holder to where they are going next, the tools and insights outlined in this social justice guide will help develop your resiliency and build your confidence enough to pursue what's next in your own social justice journey.

If you're still not sure about the red pill or just beginning your journey, here are several thoughts to spark your interest and ignite your torch:

● **You have long felt a deep desire to contribute to something larger than yourself.**

Taking the social justice journey means caring not only about the lives of others but making an impact on the larger world around you. When you commit to working toward an equitable society, you are acting in the interest of yourself and so many others. You benefit when others benefit. Just as oppression affects us all negatively, prosperity benefits everyone positively. As the old saying from John F. Kennedy goes, "a rising tide lifts all boats." When more people have jobs, the overall economy improves. When everyone is healthier, costs of healthcare go down. When there is less poverty, there is less crime. Taking the social justice journey means improving the lives of everyone, including yourself.

● **You are not content with the status quo and want to be on the right side of history.**

Martin Luther King, Jr. made this saying popular, "The arc of the moral universe is long, but it bends towards justice." History is ripe with examples of systemic oppression and devastating acts of hatred. It's also ripe with movements toward peace and empowered acts of love. Taking the social justice journey means working daily to overwhelm oppression and hatred with peace, empathy, and compassion.

● You want to become a better human being.

Working toward social justice requires one to open themselves up to perspectives and viewpoints that might be different from their own. It requires you to be honest about your own biases and ignorance. It requires you to learn and grow. As the great vocalist and actress Pearl Bailey said, "You never find yourself until you face the truth." Taking the social justice journey means you will improve and become a better person in ways that you never before considered.

● You find it increasingly difficult to remain neutral.

Sometimes when faced with a difficult decision, the easiest option is to simply do nothing. When we see injustice happening in the world it might be tempting to sit back and assume that others will act. The reality in most cases, however, is that no one acts and the injustice continues. The machine of oppression in our world is established and powerful; it will not disintegrate unless we stop conforming and instead actively resist. As historian Howard Zinn wrote in his book, *You Can't Be Neutral on a Moving Train,* "But human beings are not machines, and however powerful the pressure to conform, they sometimes are so moved by what they see as injustice that they dare to declare their independence. In that historical possibility lies hope."

So, are you ready to take the social justice journey?

The next step is deciding what shape your journey will take. The beautiful part about deciding to take this journey is that *you* get to decide what it becomes. Once you truly decide to value equity, you begin to see the world in a different way and everything will be shaped by your new perspective. You don't need to quit your job and pick up a bullhorn to be on the social justice journey, but you certainly can if that is your calling.

For some, the journey might mean having a conversation with a friend about a topic like social class or sexual orientation. For others it might mean signing up for a workshop to delve more deeply into a conversation about diversity with a group of peers. For others still, it could mean reading and then striving to live the concepts in this book.

It's important to remember that our journey is about action. As Desmond Tutu put it, ". . . doing your little bit of good where you are; it's those little bits of good put together that overwhelm the world."

If this means creating a nonprofit organization that seeks to end modern-day slavery in the supply chain of major clothing manufacturers, great. If it means planning your next vacation to go visit the National Civil Rights Museum in Memphis, great. If it means granting yourself five minutes of quiet time to reflect on your own privilege, great. All action matters, all action will improve your journey, and all action will in some way improve the world around you. This is social justice.

Chapter 2:
VITAL

*It is good to have an end to journey towards;
but it is the journey that matters in the end.*
—Ursula LeGuin

Before we dive into VITAL, let it be known: We are not social justice "experts." While we honor that you can and should be an expert on your own narrative, we don't believe there are social justice "experts." To us, social justice is about the process; it's about the mosaic of paths that come together to create the picture of how we live our lives. Countless friends, mentors, and thinkers have been our torch at various points along our social justice journey. It's with their collective spirit that we seek to serve as a torch for you. Yes, we all are striving for the targeted outcome of a truly just world, but it's the process of continuous learning, growing, and deepening our journey that allows us to sustain our collective practice.

That said, we've had the fortune of gathering some insights throughout our years of applying and tweaking our social justice concepts. And we've practiced these insights in our marriage, in countries around the globe, at Ivy League universities, and with our own families and friends. VITAL represents a synthesis of life lessons and shared wisdom that have lit the way for thousands of people to deepen their social justice journeys.

In many professional circles, the phrase "best practice" is used to describe methods or techniques that consistently produce superior results. Recognizing the increasingly diverse workplace and unique circumstances of individual groups and organizations, we have reimagined the philosophy of "best practice" and developed an original approach for social justice work. We call this VITAL.

Imagine feeling completely empowered during a conversation about social justice. Instead of being railroaded by guilt, imagine finding courage in vulnerability. Instead of getting shut down by triggers, imagine finding strength in story. Instead of tiptoeing around issues, imagine finding community in authentic dialogue. VITAL can help give you the knowledge, tools, and confidence to effectively integrate social justice into your everyday life.

Just as the yogi engages in a consistent yoga practice, social justice journeyers also develop regular patterns of thoughts and behaviors that allow them to deepen and strengthen their social justice work. When building strength in a new yoga posture, sometimes your muscles will shake and tremble. Similarly, sometimes your confidence wavers when you uncover new aspects of privilege and oppression on your social justice journey. This is okay. In fact, this is an indicator of the process and work that goes into building strength.

VITAL is the torch for your social justice journey. It is a beacon for navigating the waters of personal-growth and finding solidarity with others. Here are the tools:

VULNERABILITY

Sharing your story takes courage. Learning about yourself, including privileges, biases, triggers, and insecurities requires honesty. Vulnerability is key in building authentic relationships and communicating effectively across differences.

IDENTITY

Who we are matters. The multiple aspects of our identity, including race, gender, sexuality, social class, national origin, etc., impact our daily lives and those around us. To work effectively with others, we must understand these identities and how they influence our individual experiences, group dynamics, and social systems.

TRUST

Engaging in development, whether as an individual or in a group, requires trust. Oftentimes there is dissonance or discord in the process of learning about ourselves, our identities, systems of privilege and oppression, and practicing vulnerability. In those moments, trusting the process is important to staying connected, engaged, and open to growth.

AUTHORSHIP

Empowerment is a key component to success. If you don't feel invested and validated, you won't contribute effectively. Your story is only yours to tell. Bearing witness to someone else's story is humbling and illuminating, and having authorship in the telling of your own story is extremely powerful as it liberates the narrator and ensures voice is being given to those who may otherwise be silenced, excluded, or overlooked.

LIBERATION

Freeing ourselves from a cycle of oppression involves both unlearning the ways in which we have been socialized *and* working to dismantle oppressive systems. Liberation is a process and an outcome that depends on learning about ourselves and our society. To foster broader social impact we must start by liberating ourselves.

The VITAL practice for social justice journeying is explored in more depth over the next five chapters. Our hope is that as you learn these principles you will lean into any tensions that arise; this is the trembling of the muscle, the way to strengthen and deepen your social justice practice. We also hope you will take time to rejoice in the many improvements and adjustments you will make along your journey.

Note on Triggers: In our experience, social justice journeying can involve encountering, managing, and responding to triggers.

Triggers are emotional, psychological, and physical reactions to experiences that remind us of traumatic moments in our lives. For example, when reading about homophobia, someone could be triggered as a result of their own painful experiences with homophobia. While triggers themselves are generally regarded as negative, the experiences that bring them about are difficult to anticipate and might not have anything to do with the original trauma.

Given that we'll be discussing some sensitive topics such as social identity, privilege, and oppression, we believe it's important to acknowledge the potential for triggers along the way. As opposed to holding you back from embarking on a social justice journey, however, we believe that working through triggers can be an essential part of the process. Developing a resilience around navigating triggers is a powerful step toward liberation.

Triggers can also be sources of great healing in our lives. These traumatic memories are often indicators of fear, anxiety, and pain that continue to wound us far after the experience is over. If we can develop the tools to confront these memories when they surface, we can begin the process of healing.

Final Note: We are of the firm belief that VITAL will never be a perfect model that applies to everyone and all situations. We ask that you utilize the concepts that work for you and be open to the ones that might seem less relevant. VITAL is meant to be broad, encompassing the big-picture values of social justice for anyone, including those at the start of their journey or those well-versed in their practice. We look forward to being a part of your journey and we welcome your feedback along the way.

CHAPTER 3:
VULNERABILITY

Vulnerability sounds like truth and feels like courage.
—*Brené Brown*

Imagine yourself facing an enormous mountain. Standing at the base, you can feel the rush of wind swirling around you as you strain your neck to look up to the top of the rock face that you will soon climb. Putting on your harness and helmet, you reassure yourself that you've taken all the proper safety precautions, so there is nothing to fear. But you've never climbed a height this tall before. Sure, you have climbed lots of challenging mountains in your lifetime, but none this demanding. After double-checking all of your knots and equipment, you approach the rock wall and look over your shoulder to let your support person know that you are about to start.

You extend your arms and find sturdy holds for your hands. Lifting your right foot, you secure your toe on a large rock and lift your left foot into a crevasse near the base of the mountain. You've done it! You've officially left the ground and started your climb. With each advance up the wall, you feel your heart beat faster. Looking out to your side, you see the amazing view from where you've climbed. You can only imagine what it will feel like at the top.

After ten minutes, you look down to see how far you've come and your stomach drops, your knees weaken, and your hands begin to sweat. The confidence and strength you felt just a few minutes ago has vanished and you can't take another step. The thought crosses your mind to stop and make your way back to solid ground. Your support person on the ground yells up words of encouragement and you remember all of the safety precautions you took before starting the climb. You know you're physically safe, but you are at the edge of your comfort zone. Taking a deep breath, you muster all the courage you have and push yourself up one step higher. Then another, then another. You won't stop until you reach the top.

It took an immense amount of vulnerability to complete your climb. Not only did you have to call upon your previous knowledge and experience, you also had to rely on your support partner as well. It was a risk you determined was worth taking. You put yourself out there and were willing to be vulnerable in order to accomplish your goal.

Exploring issues of identity and diversity is a lot like rock climbing. Even if you're well-versed on these topics, they can still present challenges. Precautions for personal safety should be taken and you should have a support network to rely on, one that can give you encouragement and help your processing along the way. When moments of fear arise, assess the situation and determine if you need to pull back. Knowing the process will not be comfortable, however, you should aim to be brave. Some of the most profound learning experiences happen when we are teetering on the edge of our comfort zones. Leaning into the discomfort means embracing your learning edges, those spots where personal transformation can happen. Only by pushing through these learning edges will you climb to the top of the mountain.

We call the area of vulnerability just beyond our comfort zones *brave space*, and we believe such spaces provide opportunities for immense personal growth.

But how do we continue building our strength to be vulnerable? After all, when considering power, privilege, and systemic oppression, it's easy to become cynical. The world we live in today is full of prejudice and discrimination. The social systems that reinforce injustice have been in place for hundreds, perhaps thousands, of years. Trying to dismantle these oppressive realities can seem daunting, even impossible.

Our primary approaches to finding strength in vulnerability—Self-Work and Storysharing—make us believe that there is hope no matter how bad it seems.

After all, if prejudice can be learned through messages from the media and our families, we believe it can also be unlearned. If we don't start to change things, they might never improve. As Lao Tzu, philosopher and poet of ancient China, once wrote, "The journey of a thousand miles begins with a single step."

We believe that there is hope in the unseen end of prejudice and discrimination. We believe there is hope in the unknown elimination of oppressive systems. We believe there is hope not only in the outcome, but in each step taken during the social justice journey. We must start to change these systems somewhere and while anywhere is better than nowhere, we've found the best place to start is within ourselves.

SELF-WORK

The end goal of social justice—equity—might seem like an insurmountable height to climb. It will take effort and time. Likely far more than any of us will ever have. But that doesn't mean it isn't worth working toward, especially when we grow as individuals during the process.

Just as you felt the fear of falling but kept pushing on to stand courageously at the mountain's peak, self-work can often stir up fear as it develops. Being internally vulnerable and vulnerable with others is a way to own our imperfections while inviting others into our journey.

When thinking about the problems that exist in the world today, it is all too easy to look out and point fingers at those who we think are responsible.

Very rarely do we wonder how we may be directly or indirectly part of the problem. As Mahatma Gandhi once said, "Be the change you wish to see in the world."

The social justice journeyer wholeheartedly believes in this philosophy.

While we might not be personally responsible for the oppression that others experience, it is up to each of us to interrupt discrimination and stop hatred. Engaging in self-work means turning the mirror at ourselves to see where we can make changes toward social justice. The journey starts with developing our own awareness through a process of self-reflection.

Engaging in continued self-work—continued questioning of our own privileges and continued reflection on where we are in our journey—can be one of the most effective ways to overcome the challenges and barriers in doing social justice work. It's the process of understanding one's own identities and understanding personal attitudes and behaviors that might reinforce cycles of oppression. Informed by the work of author and researcher Brené Brown, self-work requires journeyers to be vulnerable about their own biases and areas for growth. In doing so, they can develop their capacity to be authentically true to themselves and empathic allies alongside others.

Self-work is critical to social justice because positive change starts from within. You care enough about equity and fairness to be reading this book. It's all but impossible to create meaningful change in the world if we aren't willing to evaluate our own thoughts and behaviors. By engaging in the principles of self-work, you can begin to model what change looks like and inspire others to do the same.

Expectedly, the second approach to finding strength in vulnerability, storysharing, is best shown through story.

"A Little Shady"

KYLE: When I think about the storysharing approach to vulnerability, I am reminded of my first visit to Springfield, Massachusetts. Having never been there, I sought out friends beforehand to get a sense for what to expect. One colleague, who identifies as a White woman, told me that Springfield wasn't exactly the most exciting place to visit and that many parts were "a little shady."

Upon arriving to Springfield, I found a place to eat with some friends. I asked if any of them had ever been to the area before. Many said they had and that they thought it was a medium-sized city and a good spot for conferences. I was surprised by their enthusiasm for the city, given my previous colleague's review, and so I offered my opinion to the group.

"Well, it seems pretty run down so far. I heard there are many parts that are a little shady," I said.

Without missing a beat, a friend responded with a comment that has stuck with me ever since.

"What do you mean by 'a little shady?' Do you mean that Black people live here?" she asked.

I was speechless. My stomach immediately tightened and fell to the ground. In fact I was aware that Springfield was home to mostly communities of color, but I hadn't stopped to think about the racist connotation that came with the phrase "a little shady." In that moment, I wanted to curl myself into a ball so that no one could see my shame. I wanted to run away and avoid the embarrassment of having to respond to her question. Alternatively, my first thought was about pushing back against my vulnerability rather than leaning into and learning from it. A part of me wanted to put up my dukes and get defensive about her interpretation of my words. I wanted to prove my true anti-racist character to the group.

The reality was, however, that no matter what I said or did, I couldn't take back what I had said. She was right and I knew it. The term "a little shady" did have an implicit racial bias and she was brave enough to bring that to my attention.

So instead of turning to run or engaging in a heated debate, I took a moment to let her question sink in. Then I looked her in the eyes and said, "You know what? You're right. That was a pretty racist thing to say. Thanks for calling me out."

She smiled and said, "Not a problem. I hope you give Springfield a chance. It's not such a bad place."

If I hadn't committed to a process of self-work, and if I hadn't cultivated a practice of believing in the power of vulnerability, I wouldn't have been able to learn and grow from the experience. She offered me a chance to think critically about colloquial language and the way this language can negatively impact huge communities of people. By hearing her out, I was able to see the truth in her words. If I had walked away or decided to fight, I probably wouldn't have learned anything from the exchange; I probably would've walked away more entrenched in my belief that Springfield, and by extension, other communities of color like it, are "a little shady."

Telling this story has a powerful effect on me. The simple act of sharing this story challenges me to be vulnerable, admitting a time when I made a mistake in my social justice journey. Storysharing can force us to lean into the discomfort of hard lessons learned along the way. By doing so, we are able to continue the cycle of learning and growing by sharing our insights. Through storysharing, we continue our own process of reflection and allow opportunities of reflection for others.

SIDE CROW

AERIEL: Recently in a Vinyasa Flow yoga class, we were deepening our practice by trying new inversions. I love being inverted. The shift in perspective does great things for me physically and emotionally. On mornings that I wake up on the proverbial "wrong side of the bed," spending a few minutes upside down allows me to reclaim my day and feel much better. On this particular morning, our yoga instructor was cuing us through side crow.

Having never attempted this posture before, I felt my heart begin to race with anticipation. Intently focusing on my breathing, I slowly shifted my weight onto my forearms and lightly pushed my feet off the ground. Teetering, my feet settled back down on the floor. I knew fear was holding me back. While I love being inverted, the proximity of my neck and head to the ground tends to make me a bit apprehensive. Centering my breath, I tried again—this time pushing off the ground a bit harder.

For a moment, I was there—in the elusive side crow. Fixated on a neutral focal point, I felt like I was floating! But before long, my momentum from my initial push-off coupled with the force of gravity made me topple forward. I landed on my bum next to my mat and all I could do was laugh out loud. Smiling at my progress, my yoga instructor commended me on my first side crow attempt:

"That's good! We need to laugh at ourselves as we bravely try new postures and teeter in uncomfortable spaces."

Her words of encouragement have stuck with me, and are entirely relevant to life both on and off the mat. Bravery is needed not only to lean into postures and deepen our yoga practice, but also as we embark on our social justice journey. Opening ourselves up to the possibility of falling or failure is a necessary prerequisite to growing in our practice. Kyle and I believe that brave space, an intentional pushing of oneself beyond your comfort zone, is necessary to effectively deepen and strengthen your social justice practice. The same is true for trying a new yoga posture. Finding the courage to lean into uncertainty enabled me to test my limits and fly in side crow, even if only for a few fleeting seconds.

The parallels between yoga and social justice journeying go beyond the concept of brave space. Core to our ability to authentically engage in both, is a willingness to be vulnerable.

Vulnerability in the context of social justice journeying can be framed in two parts: inner vulnerability and outer vulnerability.

Inner vulnerability is our personal willingness to confront our privileges, acknowledge our shortcomings, and engage in self-work as we seek to lean into our learning edges and deepen our understanding. Inner vulnerability is quieting the voice of doubt that says "I can't do side crow."

Outer vulnerability is a willingness to practice vulnerability with others by owning up to our mistakes, acknowledging when we don't have all the answers, and sharing stories in the pursuit of greater knowledge. Outer vulnerability is trusting your community of yoga practice to the extent that you can attempt side crow, even if that means you falter, without the fear of judgement from your fellow yogis.

What's fascinating about vulnerability—as it pertains to yoga as well as our social justice practice—is that choosing to be vulnerable creates spaces and grants permission for others to courageously be vulnerable as well. As I was teetering and tottering in and out of side crow, striving to be open to falling and laughing at myself, I saw out of the corner of my eye other yogis also working to deepen their practice. Their vulnerability and courage to bravely try new postures inspired me to lean in and continue working.

Our willingness to try new postures allows us to develop strength and confidence in our yoga practice, which enables us to deepen our physical and emotional experience.

Similarly, our willingness to engage in self-work (inner vulnerability) prepares us for the myriad ways of engaging with others, such as storysharing (outer vulnerability). Through storysharing we gain the profound experience of bearing witness to others' truths while also developing our own capacity to author our lived experiences and narratives. These experiences of digging deeper and sharing wider prompt new personal insights and continue a cyclical and deepening process of self-work in our journey.

Unintentional Outing

KYLE: Learning to lean into vulnerability often comes, for me at least, the hard way. Another example occurred when I was co-facilitating a workshop with a colleague who identifies as lesbian. The workshop was about exploring sexual orientation and sexual identity and we were in the process of introducing ourselves to the group. My intention was to give some context about myself and my identity while owning some of the privilege I have as a heterosexual-identified person.

My co-facilitator had not yet had the opportunity to introduce herself and as a result, the group did not know her sexual orientation. Without thinking, I mentioned that I had more privilege than my co-facilitator due to my heterosexual identity and her lesbian identity, which meant fewer obstacles and challenges for me over the course of my life. While I thought this acknowledgement was in line with being a good ally, I didn't think about how it might feel for her to be outed to the group by someone else. Whether or not she was planning to tell the group this information, it was not my place to share that sensitive and personal part of her identity.

After the facilitation ended, she approached me and let me know that she was disappointed in my oversight. She expected more of me as an ally. To be honest, I also expected more of myself. I immediately felt embarrassed because I knew she was right. I had made a mistake in outing her to the group without her permission. Instead of becoming defensive or trying to explain away the reasons why she shouldn't be upset, I chose to lean into my own discomfort and accept responsibility. I apologized and told her that I hadn't even thought about how my attempting to own my privilege could unintentionally take power away from her ability to share her own story. The next time we facilitated with that same group, I addressed my mistake and used it as an example of how an ally can make mistakes despite their best intentions.

When we realize that we've made mistakes and we feel the pangs of guilt and embarrassment, strength in vulnerability encourages us to sit with those feelings and explore where they come from. Through the self-work of continually analyzing these occasional red flags in our daily lives, we can work toward improving ourselves and our communities.

When Ego Drives

KYLE: A few years ago Aeriel and I were driving across the country and had been driving for several days. We were tired, hungry, and cranky. At the pinnacle of our tiredness, we noticed the low fuel light.

Instead of reading the road signs and choosing an exit that had an easy on-off gas station, I decided to take my chances at the next exit. *There has to be a gas station nearby*, I thought to myself.

After about five miles down the road, Aeriel turns to me and lovingly asks if I have any idea as to where I'm going. Unlike me, she's very intuitive with directions and knew immediately that we had gone down the wrong road. My inner voice was slowly hinting at the idea of being off course, but I wasn't about to admit that out loud.

"There's going to be a station soon. I saw a sign just a minute ago," I muttered.

I hadn't seen a sign.

"Do you want to stop and ask for directions?" Aeriel asked.

"No. I know where we're going."

I didn't know where we were going.

We ended up driving through cornfields for nearly twenty minutes before stumbling upon a gas station. By the time we reached the pump, our car was running on fumes and the mood was tense. Not an ideal situation for a road trip.

This was a situation that required me to be courageous and, unfortunately, I failed. I thought I was being courageous in trying to solve the problem on my own without help from anyone. Since then I've come to understand that the status quo definition of "courage" wasn't the one I wanted to live by.

What is the most courageous thing *you've* ever done?

Generally, we define courage by the following characteristics: strength, independence, and self-reliance. Certainly those are good characteristics, but I no longer think they have anything to do with courage.

When we think about the most courageous things we've done in our lives, they are typically actions that required us to be honest, humble, and above all, vulnerable. They required us to admit that we needed help. They required us to be willing to fail. They required us to put our ego to the side and let the chips fall where they may.

In our experience, courage and vulnerability are undeniably interconnected.

Sadly though, many still view vulnerability as a sign of weakness instead of an act of courage. Weakness is generally not an appealing quality, and as a result, many people go to very extreme lengths (as I did when lying to Aeriel about the gas station sign) to avoid demonstrating even an ounce of vulnerability.

The fear of judgement that is associated with being perceived as weak or inadequate can be paralyzing. Instead of risking that, many prefer to put up imaginary walls and avoid vulnerability altogether. Instead of leading to security and confidence, avoiding vulnerability can lead to silence, regret, and unfulfilled potential.

Roller Skating Hero

AERIEL: Early 90s pump-up jams are playing on the overhead sound system as clusters of excitable tweens giggle and gossip. They're lacing up their roller skates as they sit in oversized red plastic booth tables. A group of ultra-cool upper-class girls huddle around a high-top table just outside the arcade. They order a pizza and a pitcher of cola to share. A trio of younger boys zips around the worn forest green carpet on their rented skates, racing to scope out what their arcade tickets can buy at the prize counter.

Just then, the overly charismatic DJ with his booming cheerful voice gets on the loudspeaker and tells everyone it's time to get out onto the skating rink! He turns up the music and starts the orange, white, and blue spotlights, which bounce off and reflect light from a low-hanging disco ball in the center of the rink.

The suspense builds, but there's hesitation. No one is willing to bravely take the first step out onto the floor. People begin lining up along the railing, casually chatting with friends, scanning the crowd, and wondering who will be the first one out onto the roller skating rink.

One brave soul breaks from the crowd and unsteadily moves out onto the floor. At first everyone holds their breath, worrying and waiting to see if she falls. Taking the first few deliberate strides, our roller skating hero can practically hear her heart beating out of her chest. She's nervous knowing all eyes are on her, but the exhilaration of leading the way for her friends wins out.

She gains speed and confidence as she completes her first full loop. Smiling, she beckons to her friends to join her as she leans into the curve of the rink, and before you know it, swarms of happy pre-teens scramble out onto the floor to join in the fun.

This scene—the feeling of anticipation, suspense, and nervousness of waiting for the first person to make their way out onto the roller skating rink—is similar to thinking about vulnerability in social justice journeying. If the idea of being vulnerable, of sharing your lived experiences, and naming the ways in which you've been socialized to believe in hierarchies of identity absolutely terrifies you, think of the young girl who was the first to bravely step out onto the roller skating rink. By focusing on the group's interests rather than her own insecurities, she models vulnerability and it is through her courage that others are invited to do the same.

SHOWING UP IS NOT ENOUGH

KYLE: I was in a room with fifty other people for a social justice conference. For four days, this diverse group talked about race and its many dimensions. Growing up in a White family in rural Michigan, I was raised not to talk about race. In fact, I was so privileged that I did not have to talk about race because everyone around me was White and we all benefitted from this. If the topic ever did come up, it was alluded to and would be about how dangerous it was to travel to the neighboring town because "those people" lived there.

Originally, I signed up for the conference because I had several mentors recommend it as a good opportunity to learn and grow. They never mentioned anything about how terrifying it would be. Each morning I walked into the conference room with a tense knot in my stomach. I was petrified because I didn't want to say anything that others in the group might interpret as racist or offensive.

On the last morning of the conference, my nightmare became a reality. Everyone in the group stood in a large circle and the White people were invited to voluntarily step forward and talk about a time when they said or did something racist. As the activity went on, I listened to others bravely admit the very thing that I was desperately trying to avoid. My heart began to race and the knot in my stomach tightened.

In the end, my fear got the best of me and I chose not to participate. I failed the group and myself because I was afraid of being judged. I was afraid of being perceived as inadequate.

After talking with people who did share their experiences, I realized I had to get over trying to be perfect. Just showing up to the conversation was not enough. Being a true ally in social justice work demands owning my imperfections and being honest with others about them. In doing so, I could work to unlearn the oppressive assumptions I have been socialized to believe throughout my life.

Through this experience I discovered vulnerability as a path toward allyship as well as a way to heal my insecurities, flaws, and fears. I also learned that confronting my privilege, bias, and triggers is an essential part of growing through vulnerability.

Self-work, this process of examining one's own identities in relation to systems of privilege and oppression, forces us to be vulnerable and to find value in that vulnerability. Laying your fears, shame, insecurity, and pain on the table can be terrifying, but it is the only way to start healing. Being honest about our own areas for growth, especially related to privilege and bias, is a powerful step toward fostering personal transformation and creating social justice.

In its simplest form, vulnerability is about being authentic, honest, and humble. It's about sharing your hopes, fears, joys, and insecurities with those that you trust and hope to develop deep relationships with. It's about being honest with yourself and others about your strengths and areas for growth. It's about admitting when you have made mistakes and acknowledging the possibility of other truths.

Being vulnerable is also about stepping up and stepping into conversations that might be uncomfortable but are essential in order to strengthen and deepen relationships.

INSIDE OUT

AERIEL: Growing up I would sometimes joke that the familiar Sesame Street song that goes, "one of these things is not like the other..." could be a running soundtrack for my life. I'm a transracial adoptee, which means that I am Asian and was raised by a White family. As a transracial adoptee, I was the only Korean face in my family portraits, and so I sometimes felt like the odd one out. Unsure of how to navigate the nuances of my racial identity as a transracial adoptee, I often fell back on humor as a way to navigate what otherwise felt like overly complex issues.

It was a running joke among high school friends that I was like a Twinkie—yellow on the outside and white on the inside.

In fact, it wasn't until graduate school that I began to really do some reflecting and self-work around my racial identity as a transracial adoptee. This included practicing inner vulnerability as I began to unpack and name the ways in which I felt different growing up.

My racial identity journey was never about pointing fingers or placing blame, rather it was about trying to understand why and how I developed my own sense of self as an Anderson and as an Asian American.

It was through my graduate coursework that I first learned about scholar Bobbie Harro's cycle of socialization, and in the process of exploring my own racial identity I came to regularly practice inner vulnerability by leaning into areas of discomfort. For me, that meant leaning into my learning edges around internalized racism. Instead of naively asserting a claim to Whiteness given my transracial adoption (and trivializing this racial and cultural blurring of borders with jokes about being a Twinkie or a banana) I began to critically consider how messages I received growing up informed my understanding, connection to, and performance of an Asian identity.

Graduate school was also a profound time to engage in outer vulnerability. To storyshare with and among my classmates allowed parts of my psyche to blossom in ways I didn't expect.

We were all on our own transformative racial identity journeys. Our willingness to vulnerably share some of our obstacles, fears, and insecurities—as well as the power of bearing witness to one another's stories of critical race incidents—was a dynamic experience in outer shared vulnerability.

I remember one poignant example when a biracial classmate confessed that she imagined the person who had broken into her car the night before to be a Black man. This peer's vulnerability in sharing her own racial biases was triggering for some, but also created brave space for others to admit similar examples of racial socialization. By authentically and vulnerably sharing her own internalized racial biases—by openly sharing with us her self-work journey—this classmate role modeled outer vulnerability in a way that empowered the rest of us to critically consider our own socializations and internal biases.

TIME AND PLACE

AERIEL: We have established that vulnerability is a key practice to fostering authentic relationships across differences. Some readers may be wondering, *But is it always appropriate to practice vulnerability?*

Perhaps you work in an environment that thrives on competition and doesn't value vulnerability. Or maybe the culture of your home neighborhood or community doesn't allow for vulnerability and views that sort of emotional transparency as weakness. Without a doubt there is an element of time and place for practicing vulnerability. You will need to consider your audience, your safety, and your intentions when being vulnerable on your journey.

FLOODLIGHTING

Another consideration when strategizing when and how to be vulnerable is the all too familiar "overshare." We've all been in this type of situation when one group member goes far deeper than anyone else, sharing much more intimate details and or information. In some ways, a pouring out of emotion can be an exemplary showing of vulnerability. However, as Brené Brown explains in her book,

Daring Greatly, we need to be judicious with whom to share our vulnerability.

Vulnerability is to be earned and shared appropriately. Story dumping, the act of verbally vomiting on someone without an established foundation, can actually have the opposite effect of what is desired. Rather than strengthening a relationship, floodlighting can stop a relationship from forming.

People can be turned off by the overshare and made wholly uncomfortable or disoriented about how to engage and respond. For example, many of us may be familiar with the ubiquitous posts on Facebook that share far too much personal information given the public nature of social media. When friends or family make such posts, they are putting themselves out there in an extremely vulnerable way and hoping for support or validation from others. There are times when this type of sharing is appropriate, but very often it can push others away due to a lack of personal connection shared through the online format.

When considering one's emotional safety and well-being, it's important to be hesitant and judicious with practicing vulnerability rather than being overly liberal and excessive with sharing personal or intimate information.

CO-OPTING

The second consideration we want to mention when practicing vulnerability is to reflect upon your intention for sharing. What is the value added? This honest reflection keeps us accountable to taking up only the space that is necessary. While, generally speaking, vulnerability begets vulnerability, this has limits.

For example, you may have a friend who comes to you with a personal challenge that they are currently struggling with in their life. In an attempt to show compassion, you explain how you too have had a similar problem. You go on to describe how you felt and what you did. Pretty soon, the conversation has unintentionally shifted from focusing on your friend to completely on you. Many of us may have similar stories to this kind of well-intended co-opting.

When one person or group co-opts a sharing space or floodlights, they shift the focus from utilizing vulnerability to deepen relationships and instead make the space all about themselves. This redirects vulnerability not for the greater good of the group, but for the voice and ego of one.

RISKS

KYLE: Judgement is by far one of the biggest risks associated with vulnerability. We often limit ourselves because we are afraid of what others might think. Our desire to fit in often trumps our desire to be completely authentic, which means we tend to say or do what we think will result in approval from others instead of what we actually desire. Fear of judgement is a compelling barrier that keeps us from vulnerability, and sometimes for good reason.

When we think of being judged, it is all too easy to recall images of high school teenagers at the lunch table nitpicking outfits and hairdos. The reality, however, is that people judge others in all sorts of situations and those judgements can sometimes have significant consequences.

From hiring practices to housing approvals, snap judgements can determine the fate of someone's life. That being said, it is understandable that some people take great caution when revealing their personal thoughts, feelings, and stories with others. This can be especially true for those who have had their vulnerable information used against them.

When we share our true selves with others—the good, bad, and ugly stuff we only tell those we trust the most—we do so in the hopes that we will be accepted and embraced. Unfortunately, however, there are times when that vulnerability is not appreciated and is even used to cause us pain. For many people, judgement represents the epitome of rejection and the sense of not belonging.

In *Daring Greatly*, Brené Brown says, ". . . true belonging only happens when we present our authentic, imperfect selves to the world, our sense of belonging can never be greater than our level of self-acceptance."

What's the difference between fitting in and belonging? Vulnerability.

When vulnerability is not reciprocated, we tend to retreat further and further into our shells. We begin believing that we aren't worthy of belonging. We begin doubting ourselves. We may even start internalizing previous judgements and inflict the feelings of rejection and pain upon ourselves. It is understandable that many become cautious about sharing their vulnerable authentic selves with others given the high-risk of judgement and self-doubt that can follow.

In order to avoid these potentially painful feelings, Brown tells us that we instead try to fit in. We build up our walls and put on our masks; we hide our whole selves from others in hopes that we can "fit in" to meet others' expectations. We aim to be liked instead of valued. This means we might say things we wouldn't normally say, or do things we might not normally do. Generally, fitting in means we are trying to be someone other than ourselves.

When we try to fit in, we suppress our true selves and avoid vulnerability at all costs. On the other hand, when we practice vulnerability with those that we trust, it can lead to true belonging.

On the surface, the risks of fitting in seem much lower than those associated with vulnerability and true belonging. The reality, however, is that invulnerability comes with significant and long-term risks.

THE BOX

KYLE: Imagine in your mind a sturdy box made of solid oak wood. Its walls are thick and impenetrable. Due to its precise dimensions and exact size, only certain objects can fit inside the box. Things that do not meet the exact dimensions of the box must remain outside. The box provides safety and comfort for the things that can fit inside. The things outside the box are independent and vulnerable.

This wooden box represents how many of us feel about fitting in with others. There are specific expectations and precise guidelines for how one should behave in order to be accepted. Knowing that we have to meet these exact dimensions in order to fit in the box we attempt to change ourselves and, accordingly, adjust who we are.

Sadly, very few of society's boxes are inclusive enough to account for all the different varieties of people and identities among us.

In his TED Talk "A Call to Men," Tony Porter provides an example showing how men are taught to be tough and stoic. This includes showing little to no emotion or concern for others. As a result, many of us stuff our feelings inside and put on a hard mask in order to convince the world we fit inside the walls of masculinity. When we realize that the dimensions of the man box are far too limiting, we take drastic and sometimes dangerous action in order to maintain the perception of manhood. Soaring rates of high-risk behavior among men, from substance abuse to violence, are in large part a result of the rules many men feel they need to follow in order to stay in the man box to fit in.

Placing such strict limitations on ourselves can lead to inauthenticity and ultimately regret.

HUNTING FOR APPROVAL

KYLE: I grew up in rural Michigan. Every year when deer season came around my dad would beam with excitement. He would carefully set up a deer decoy in the backyard and have me stand with him for hours as he target practiced. He even bought me a tiny child-sized bow in candy-apple red so that I could practice along with him.

I love my dad very much and I greatly appreciate his efforts to include me in his personal passions. Looking back, I know that I was lucky to have a dad that wanted to spend that much time with me.

But I was never really that interested in hunting. Sure, I enjoyed target practice because it was a fun skill that somewhat resembled a video game, but the thought of actually killing a living animal terrified me.

Before I was old enough to go out to the woods with my dad, he would come home from his autumn hunts with a prize buck in the back of his truck. Thick smears of blood would stain the truck bed, and the animal would resemble a lifeless monster when it swiveled from a suspended rope in our dimly lit garage. The last thing I wanted to do was venture off into the wilderness in search of these frightening creatures. Additionally, I had no idea what it meant to take an animal's life. The thought of killing anything, let alone a deer twice my size, threw me into a fit of anxiety and confusion.

Despite my aversion to the actual implications of hunting, however, I never communicated my feelings with my dad. His passion for the activity was profound and I worried that my disinterest would disappoint him, leading him to be disappointed in me as his son. The last thing I wanted was for my dad to be disappointed in me, so I did what many of us do when we are trying to fit in. I bottled up my feelings to try to make him happy.

When I was around sixteen years old, I joined my dad on a hunting trip as I did many times before, but this time I was equipped with a rifle. We would typically bow hunt, but he was excited to have me try something new. After a few hours sitting in the cold and silent woods, a doe approached our tree stand. My dad looked me in the eyes and gave me the encouraging nod to take the shot. Uncertain of what to do and not wanting to disappoint him, I closed my eyes and squeezed the trigger.

As I opened my eyes and saw the animal lying limp on the ground, my stomach sank. The realization that I had taken a life became real and I immediately felt a sense of shame. My dad, on the other hand, was ecstatic at my very first kill. He rushed to the animal, checked to make sure it was dead and then gave me the thumbs up.

After that, hunting was never really the same for us. I did go with him a few more times, but he could tell that something had changed inside me. I never said anything to him, but I stopped wanting to practice shooting my bow and came up with excuses when he wanted to head out to the woods. Eventually he stopped asking me to join him and that part of our relationship faded.

Thinking back, I still feel a sense of regret because I killed that deer. Don't get me wrong. I have profound respect for hunters who take it upon themselves to connect with nature in order to provide food for themselves and their families. This critical moment in my life revealed that I am not a hunter. I simply don't have the ability to take the life of another living animal. Even though I was just a young boy, I wish I could have been more honest and vulnerable with my dad about this realization. I wish I could have told him how I felt about hunting. I wish I could have been my authentic self without having to worry about disappointing him.

I don't blame him for any of those remorseful feelings. Like many young men, I was confused about who I was and was trying hard to fit in. Unfortunately, that confusion had an impact on my relationship with him. As I grow older and make meaning of my childhood, I realize the importance of working to grow our relationship in other ways.

This story of trying to fit in and make my dad happy is just one example of how inauthenticity can result in regret. For many, the lasting implications of not being our true selves leave deep wounds. The fears and insecurities that many of us carry throughout our lives often stem from times when we have neglected our authentic feelings in order to gain approval. Our pain ends up limiting the depth of our relationships and holding us back from reaching our full potential. These scars of internalized shame can lead to unhealthy lifestyle choices in order to cope with the pain we feel as a result. No wonder our country is often cited as one of the most highly medicated, caffeinated, and sexualized nations in the world.

The good news is that we don't have to be trapped by our wounds. Just as invulnerability can lead to insecurity, vulnerability can result in confidence and empowerment. Confronting our shame with honesty and vulnerability can allow us to heal. Sharing our true selves with those we trust enables us to move forward and thrive.

ON LAST NAMES

KYLE: After our engagement in 2012, Aeriel and I started planning for our wedding, which included determining our married names. Before the wedding, my full name was Kyle Lee Carpenter and her full name was Aeriel Ashley Anderson. Traditionally, the woman would take the man's last name, but this custom seemed incongruent with our social justice values.

I didn't believe that I should get to keep my last name just because I was a man. Additionally, the tradition of having the woman in a heterosexual relationship take the man's last name is a custom established on the archaic idea that upon marriage a woman becomes the man's property. Neither I nor Aeriel believed in this tradition and certainly didn't want values of ownership and patriarchy to be reflected in our married name.

After deciding we would not have Aeriel take my last name, we started exploring the various options. Like many couples who come to a similar conclusion, we thought about hyphenating our last name, which would have been Carpenter-Anderson or Anderson-Carpenter. The length alone was enough to deter us, but also a deterrent was the idea of forcing our hypothetical future children to awkwardly and painfully try to fit a name with so many characters into a standardized test bubble sheet.

Next we turned to combining our last names to create a new family name. This proved to be more of a challenge than we anticipated. Going around in circles for several months through different combinations and variations, we finally decided that there was not a pleasant sounding way to combine our last names. Nearly every option sounded like a species of fish, which wasn't what we were hoping for.

In the end, we decided to form our new family name by combining our middle names. My middle name, Lee, was significant in that it was passed down to me from my father who also shared the same middle name. Aeriel's middle name, Ashley, was important for her because the initials of her Korean given name are ASH. Combining these two to create the name Ashlee, we discovered a wonderfully creative name that aligned with our values of equity and respect.

Deciding on a name was only half the battle. I feared that deviating from tradition would not be popular with my family. I worried that my parents would not understand our reasons for creating a new family name. Additionally, I was concerned they might take it personally as a sign that I did not appreciate the Carpenter family name. I was socialized to believe that the man is traditionally supposed to carry on the family name and my decision would directly contradict this expectation. Aeriel's family might also find the decision different and slightly strange, but I worried the real resistance would be from my family.

I finally broke the news to my family, which led to several challenging conversations about the decision to change my name. In the months leading up to the wedding, there was tension and conflict between me and the rest of my family. Even on the day of the wedding there were tears shed about my decision to break away and start a new family name.

Years later, the topic of the name change is still a sensitive one in my family, but it led to honest conversations that developed stronger relationships between me, Aeriel, and my family. In addition, Aeriel and I have a last name that we are proud of. When we tell the story of our last name to people we meet, we beam with excitement because it was an innovative idea that allowed us to live out our values.

Being courageous through vulnerability has the potential to lead to healthier relationships, stronger communities, and incredibly innovative ideas. In fact, as Brené Brown explains, creativity and innovation are by their very nature acts of vulnerability. To think beyond the bounds of what has already been done and create a vision for something larger is inherently risky. New ideas are often met with opposition and resistance. A willingness to vulnerably persevere through these challenges is often the most important factor in developing new technologies, improving medicine and health care, and fostering stronger social and political systems.

In addition to broad innovations, vulnerability can lead to creative personal improvements at the individual level. This can then open the door and give love a chance to shine.

Making the decision to create our own family name was courageous and brave. We anticipated we might get pushback and resistance. We knew we would have to be vulnerable and take some risks. But doing so allowed us to think outside the box and create a solution that would otherwise have been impossible.

Fear of judgement and the innate human desire to fit in could have led us to being inauthentic and ultimately frustrated with making a decision that the status quo valued but that our collective social justice journey did not.

As the years have passed since this decision, we've found that the lasting positive impact of vulnerability has helped us. We have developed the strong foundation necessary to lead healthier lives as individuals and as a couple.

VITAL PRACTICE: VULNERABILITY

Here are some concrete examples of how you can incorporate the first tenet of VITAL—Vulnerability—into your social justice journey:

- Admit when you don't know something. In social justice conversations, sometimes terms and ideas are shared, with which you may not be familiar. Instead of nodding your head and going along with the conversation in an effort to save face, vulnerably name that which you do not know so you can actively contribute to your own learning.

- Identify and write out a list of people in your life whom you trust, and with whom you can dare to embark alongside for your social justice journey. Taking the time to name these people will equip you with an identified network of support for those challenging moments along the way.

- Reach out across differences and start a dialogue with someone you might not normally speak to. Whether it's a casual chat with a colleague of a different perceived race over lunch or a phone call to a family member you've lost touch with, sometimes the path to a new relationship connected by social justice just needs someone to take the first brave step.

- Apologize when you make a mistake. Part of social justice journeying is learning by doing, and as such there is the possibility of unintentionally hurting others along the way. A powerful act of vulnerability is to acknowledge when we have done something (even accidentally) that has caused harm to someone else. In order to work towards repairing these relationships, we may have to apologize for something we've done. You will be surprised how far those two simple words—I'm sorry—can go, when offered with sincerity.

Chapter 4:
Identity

The way in which we think of ourselves has everything to do with how our world sees us.
—Arlene Raven

Before we delve into identity, a few acknowledgments are worth exploring in regards to our approach to this topic. Identity is a complex issue and we believe it serves us well to address our understanding of it in order to establish a solid foundation moving forward.

Race and Gender Lens

First, this chapter will focus mostly on examples from the social identity categories of race and gender. While identity is extremely complex and all dimensions influence each other, we have decided—given our own personal identities and what has been salient in our social justice journey—to focus the scope of this chapter on the intersection of race and gender. We can most confidently speak to race and gender as they are the categories that have most influenced our lives.

By "social identity" we mean identities such as race, gender, sexuality, spirituality, age, socioeconomic status, and ability status, to name a few. We call these the Diversity Seven Plus or D7+, and we'll refer to them throughout this chapter.

Libraries of scientific research and anthropological analysis have shown us that many of these categories, like race and gender, have been created by people rather than biology. Society has constructed them over time in order to segregate groups into different classifications. Certainly people have different skin tones and physical body parts, but these biological characteristics are independent of the social expectations society has ascribed to them.

Social identity, as used in this context, is the set of cultural values we place on the D7+ categories. While these cultural values have been imagined by the mind, they have had very real and significant consequences for many throughout history.

Simply spanning the pages of a U.S. history textbook will give you a brief glimpse into how these social identities have impacted millions of lives. From slavery and the Civil War to women's suffrage and gay rights, the past of the United States is littered with strife over social identity. Looking beyond the narrow scope of America's borders, one can look back over centuries and see the impact of social identity around the globe.

PRIVILEGE AND OPPRESSION EXIST

We live in a world that assigns power to certain people whether by birth, title, or classification. Power, as we understand it, is the opportunity to make decisions and to have access to the resources to make those decisions. Those who have power are privileged. They have the freedom to influence their own destiny in a way others do not.

NO POWER WITHOUT PRIVILEGE

If there are those who have power, or privilege, there are also those who do not have power. To varying degrees these people are more limited in their opportunity to make decisions and tend to have significantly fewer resources. Many use the term "underprivileged" when referring to those without power, which is technically true. Following the path of scholars like bell hooks and Paulo Freire, we prefer to use the term oppression as it more clearly articulates the harsh reality experienced by those without power.

The conversation thus far has been about power, privilege, and oppression at the societal level. Certainly everyone experiences instances of opportunity or discrimination at different times in their lives. Some of these can be attributed to the specific context of a situation while others can only be explained by a larger system.

When talking about social identity and the D7+, we believe that some social identity categories provide systemic power and privilege. For example, most heterosexual couples have had the right to marry their preferred partner for centuries. Another example of systemic privilege is a man's right to vote and own land, which has been the case for most since the founding of the United States.

Conversely, we believe that other social identity categories are systematically oppressed. For example, Black Americans were not considered free from slavery until the Emancipation Proclamation of 1863 and did not have equal rights until the Civil Rights Act of 1964. Those 100 years saw laws and policies that limited access to power for African Americans that can still be felt today. Another salient example of systemic oppression has been the exclusion of women's political participation in the United States. Women were not allowed to vote in the U.S. until 1920. This late start to civic engagement has had a drastic impact. Today's 114th Congress includes only 20% women and our country has never seen a female president.

PREJUDICE, DISCRIMINATION, AND OPPRESSION

A lot of times words like prejudice, discrimination, and oppression get thrown around interchangeably in conversation. While undoubtedly related, these words have different meanings and their distinctions illustrate the levels of injustice.

Prejudice relates to the thoughts that we have about certain categories of people. Generally, these opinions are unfavorable and are formulated before we experience an actual person from those identity groups. Most prejudice is informed from messages we receive in the media, from family members, or from our communities.

Discrimination is prejudice in action. It goes beyond thoughts and translates our negative opinions into behaviors. When we discriminate, we consciously or unconsciously act on our prejudicial thought. This may result in favoring certain groups of people over others or actively excluding others based on their identities. Discrimination can be intentional or unintentional, but the impact is always harmful for those on the receiving end.

Oppression goes one step further. It represents the larger systems that allow prejudice and discrimination to continue. Similarly to privilege, oppression is about power and a lack of opportunity and resources. Oppression impacts communities as well as cultures. It results from laws, policies, or doctrines that benefit one group of people over another. The larger impact of oppression can be segregation or an unequal distribution of resources.

POSITIONALITY

AERIEL: Just as one's position on a chessboard influences the player's ability to effectively win a match, Kyle and I know that our positions in the world influence our perspectives and ability to affect change in society. As such, we believe it is important to name and acknowledge our social identities as context for the thoughts, insights, and reflections we share about our social justice journeying.

Kyle identifies as a White, cisgender, heterosexual man. These identities afford him numerous intersecting and unearned privileges. For example, the term cisgender implies that his gender identity (what he feels on the inside) matches with his biological body parts (what is seen on the outside), which is a privilege compared to those who identify as transgender. As a result of privileges like these, he believes it is his responsibility to do his own work around power, privilege, and oppression in addition to engaging other folks with privileged identities in social justice.

I identify as a heterosexual, cisgender, transracial adoptee womyn of color. Throughout this book I will use the term womyn instead of women as a political statement, indicating my preference to identify myself without having to rely on men. These social identities are the ones I think of first, the identities that most strongly influence the lens through which I see the world, and thus most powerfully impact how I experience and approach my social justice journey.

Our differing social identities, in conjunction with our marriage and commitment to center social justice in our life partnership, greatly impacts our unique perspective on working toward social justice across differences.

Additionally, Kyle and I both identify as spiritual, young professionals, upper-middle class, highly educated, and currently able-bodied. These identities position us in a way that allows us to speak from first-person perspective on some topics related to social justice and may also sometimes limit our ability to understand the lived experiences of communities we do not belong to. This is why it is so important to embark on your social justice journey with a community of support. We cannot possibly know the experience of every diverse identity group, but we do have a responsibility to name and acknowledge how our own identities shape our understanding and then intentionally reach out across differences to find others who can help guide, shape, and share their knowledge.

WHAT IS IDENTITY?

AERIEL: Who are you? Such a seemingly simple question. One that we encounter regularly at networking events, in business meetings, and when meeting new friends for the first time. Who are you?

Whenever I think of this question, the first thing that comes to mind is my name:

[I am Aeriel A. Ashlee].

Then my mind wanders to the relationships I have:

[I am a wife, I am a daughter, I am an educator].

Then I begin to think about the way others perceive me:

[I am Asian, I am a cisgender womyn, I am young].

I also consider the identities that are most salient to me:

[I am a transracial adoptee, I am a Minnesotan, I am an entreprenuer].

Of course my hobbies, interests, and passions surface as well:

[I am a tea drinker, cat lover, yogi]. . .

as do my core values:

[I am a social justice educator and a journeying-
Christian].

I find it both fascinating and humbling how three seemingly simple words, "Who are you?" can lead to such profound personal reflections. As we continue on our social justice journey of VITAL, we want to hone in on this question of identity.

Identity is complex and multifaceted. For the sake of VITAL, we are going to consider personal and social identities as two distinct although very interconnected aspects of one's life. Personal identity refers to the unique and individualized aspects of who we are. This includes our interests, hobbies, and personality characteristics. Social identities are how we show up in categories such as race and gender.

Both personal and social identities are important and interrelated. My assertive personality has implications for me as a cisgender womyn, and vice versa. Our identity options are infinite, but again, for the sake of VITAL, let's consider the D7+ primary categories of social identity. Who we are is much more complex than these seven identity boxes, and thus the plus in "D7+" is so important.

However, the D7+ in identity exploration provides a starting point. Whether or not we have considered each of these social identity categories, we show up in all of them. Beginning to explore our own social identities allows us to more deeply engage with the question, "Who are you?" which in turn informs the question, "How do you relate to and understand others?"

IDENTI-TREE

AERIEL: In my years as a social justice educator, I have found that sometimes referencing a visual concept can help illuminate the nuances and complexities of identity exploration. Allow me to introduce the "identi-tree."

Similar to the breathtaking majesty of a large old tree, exploring who we are and how our identities shape the way we walk through the world can be both humbling and overlooked. In the spring of 2009, I visited my cousin in California and we took a drive out to Muir Woods. Having grown up in the Midwest, I was familiar with the greenery of a blooming spring. I had seen seemingly infinite trees—deciduous and coniferous, old trees and saplings. In truth I had taken them for granted. It was not until this crisp March morning that I had my breath taken away by the enormity and natural power of something as familiar as trees. It was startling. How could something so commonplace—something I had seen hundreds of times before—look so different?

I have found identity exploration to be similarly awe-inspiring. Understanding who we are, the same face we see in the mirror every day, may seem like an unnecessary exercise that borders on the edge of vanity. However, the intentional journey of social identity exploration is like taking the first step into the Redwood Forest. All of a sudden the context changes. You're not just staring at your familiar reflection in the mirror; you're considering how you, as an individual tree, fit into the forest of society. Indeed, perspective has the power to shape our worldview.

Our values and our family are our roots. They are where we find nutrients and what we grow up and out of. Our branches are our many complex and varied social identities: spiritual, upper-middle class, cisgender womyn. Each branch, if examined in isolation, would be full of its own unique characteristics and qualities, each with an important story to tell. In the same way, every person who identifies as spiritual, or upper-middle class, or as a cisgender womyn has their own unique lived experience, their own stories to tell. The leaves of trees change colors with the season, and in this same way, our identities are fluid throughout life. Different contexts, settings, and environments may cause the salience of our identities to shift or altogether change.

Though my mom and dad are divorced, they have always shared a bond as naturalists and tree-huggers. They instilled in me a great love and admiration for nature. I remember my mom showing me the ringed lines of a fallen stump, and the two of us counting together the years of life the tree had witnessed. When I was in high school, my dad's property withstood a major storm that fell many trees.

With love and tenderness, he cultivated art out of tragedy by stripping the bark off the fallen trees, staining them and creating beautiful natural arches. My eldest niece swears she's going to get married underneath one. I've learned from my hippie parents that every tree has its own story to tell, and I've come to believe that every person has their own story to tell as well.

Making Soup

KYLE: I love to cook and one of my favorite things to prepare is soup. Not only do you get huge portions that can be enjoyed over time, you can also make some extremely delicious and filling meals. A soup can be incredibly complex with multiple flavor profiles and textures. It can be smooth and creamy or chunky and brothy. Regardless of what ends up in the bowl, there is no doubt that every pot of soup is ultimately determined by its unique blend of ingredients, resulting in a beautiful melody of flavors.

In some ways I believe people are similar to soups. We each have our own unique flavor profile, which is developed from the many different ingredients that make up our lives. The many identities we hold and the life experiences we've accumulated result in a harmony of expression that represents who we are and what we value.

One of the beautiful parts of a complex soup is that only the chef truly knows what goes into the finished dish. The casual diner might taste chicken noodle and decipher the main ingredients, such as chicken, pasta, carrots, celery, and broth. Some might even be able to taste the parsley and oregano that went into creating the final flavors. Ultimately, however, only the creator of the soup knows the precise amount of each ingredient and the hidden gems, like hot sauce and lime juice, that make this particular soup truly one of a kind.

The same can be said for people. Only we know the many different identities and life experiences that contribute to our personal story. On the surface, the world around us may see our gender or our racial identity and may know of some of our personal experiences. Some might even know of the deeper identities such as spirituality or national origin. But we are the only ones who know our own full story. We know the identities that are most important to our life's recipe and the ones that others may deem as more or less significant.

This is the difference between personal identity and social identity. Nearly all identities we hold are personal in some way, but social identities are generally the ones that get listed in the national census or in the standardized test boxes we check. As mentioned previously, these social identities include race, gender, sexuality, age, religion/spirituality, ability status, and socioeconomic class, among others.

These seven main social identity categories make up the parts of our identity that people and society generally consider first. They are like the chicken and noodle ingredients of our chicken noodle soup recipe. These are very important parts of our life recipe and for many of us they are the most important aspects of our identity.

However, we understand that there are many other ingredients that have gone into making us who we are and these are usually the parts of our lives that others may not see right away. The "plus" in the D7+ accounts for these other, more personal aspects of our identities, and could include identities like being a father, speaking French as a primary language, or being a small business owner.

Just as soup is a delicate balance of ingredients, our own identity ingredients interact and play off each other to result in an individual life story. When making a soup, just a few drops of one ingredient can change the flavor of the entire dish. Similarly with people, a single aspect of identity—such as national origin, ability status, or language—might seem minor but in fact can make a significant impact on who we are and how we experience the world.

Identity is extremely complex and the ways in which multiple identities intersect with one another provides for a much more comprehensive picture of a whole person. Instead of picking out the single ingredients in a soup and tasting them individually, it is much more fulfilling to appreciate the entire dish by taking time to savor the many flavors in the bowl.

As a child growing up I learned nearly everything I know about the kitchen from my mother. When my brothers would chase me inside from their big kid games of basketball with their friends, I would cling to her legs as she prepared some delicious creation bubbling on the stovetop. On the coldest Michigan winter days, she would nearly always be stirring a pot of her famous chicken noodle soup. No matter how many times she's told me the recipe, I can never quite get it to taste the way it did when she chopped the vegetables and poured in the spices herself.

Sniffing the unforgettable aroma made from my mother's loving hands, I learned a valuable lesson that goes far beyond how to make a bowl of soup. She taught me that every recipe tastes a little different, depending on who is cooking. The difference is in the unique combination of ingredients that varies from bowl to bowl and person to person.

A similar sentiment can be made about identity. Obviously an individual's identity is far more nuanced than any soup. But this simplified example has helped many shed light upon a complex concept. What can be said with certainty is that each one of us is entirely unique and our many intersecting identities help shape the way we see and experience our lives.

SALIENCE

KYLE: Context matters. At any given point in time, depending on context, different aspects of our identity become more or less important to us. The lens of identity we see the world through can change as a result of the people we are surrounded with and the places in which we find ourselves. In one moment, our gender identity may be the most important aspect of our identity and in the next moment, circumstances might change, resulting in a shifted focus on sexual orientation.

Other times, such as when we are in the zone preparing a meal, we might not even be aware of the identity that is impacting our experience. Just as we might not be able to list all of the ingredients that make up a complex recipe, it can sometimes be difficult to name the identity category that is most influencing the way we see the world. For this reason, we refer to this dynamic as "salience of identity" rather than "importance of identity." Generally when we call something important, we are fully conscious of the reason. Salience, on the other hand, indicates a factor that has a significance regardless of our awareness.

Imagine you have eight note cards in your hand. Each note card has a different identity category written on it, including race/ethnicity, gender, sexuality, religion/spirituality, socioeconomic class, ability status, age, and nationality. As you shuffle the cards around in your hands, you consider your own identity in each of these categories. Because the cards are separate, you also conceptualize each of these identities independently from the others, understanding that they do in fact influence each other in significant ways.

Next, imagine that you are asked to set down the one card or identity category that is the most salient to you at this exact moment in time. Of course, this would be an extremely challenging task, but thinking about the context—the people surrounding you and the place you find yourself in—you are able to pick one card. Envision setting that card on the floor in front of you.

From here you are asked to select the second most salient identity category for you at this moment. Again, you find it difficult to choose one over the others because they are all important to you in some way, but you are able to identify the next card and place it in front of the first card on the floor. With each round of selection, the choice becomes slightly easier and by the end you have eight cards laid out in front of you on the floor. The card closest to you is your most salient identity right now and the one farthest away from you is your least salient identity.

Think for a moment about the order of the cards in front of you. Why is the card closest to you the most salient for you right now? Is there something about the people around you that makes this identity more relevant than the others? Is there something unique about your environment that makes this identity more influential than the others? What about the card farthest away from you? Why is that identity category less salient than the others at this time, with these people, and in this place? What if you had been asked to rank the cards in order of your identity categories that are salient for others? Would the order be different if you were asked which of your identities tend to be the most or least considered by other people?

Proud to be an American

KYLE: I'm proud to be an American, but my national identity hasn't always been something that I've thought about in my daily life. I grew up in a small Midwest town and was always surrounded by people that looked like me. As such, I didn't have much of an appreciation for the wide world beyond the shores of the Great Lakes. In high school, I had the opportunity to travel to Costa Rica for a biology class field trip, which sparked my interest in learning about different countries and cultures around the world. Throughout the years, I was privileged enough to travel to a few other spots around the globe, including my time living and working in Europe.

While living abroad certainly heightened my awareness of nationality, it wasn't until my travels throughout Asia that this came to be a salient identity for me. In January of 2015, Aeriel and I embarked upon a five-month journey around the world. We were working for a college study abroad program that visits twelve different countries throughout Asia, Africa, and the United Kingdom. The trip would be my first time traveling in Asia, and the country on my passport came to mean something more significant than it had before we left.

As a United States citizen, I enjoy global privileges that many others around the world do not have. The U.S. ranks among the best countries for visa-free travel, only behind Finland, Sweden, and the United Kingdom. I can be fairly certain that no matter where I am in the world there is likely an embassy somewhere nearby that would come to my aid if I found myself in trouble. Additionally, with the relative strength of the U.S. dollar, I have greater purchasing power around the world than those from many other nations.

Geopolitics aside, and though the U.S. has its own deeply devastating problems such as economic inequality and mass incarceration, our citizens seem to enjoy a level of privilege and have access to a level of basic human rights and healthcare that are unknown to many other countries around the world.

While traveling in Southeast Asia, I witnessed a depth of poverty that is much more difficult to find traveling in the States. I saw garbage piled high in the streets, crumbling buildings, stray dogs, and sickening pollution. I visited families that lived in a two-room shack with no running water and a dirt floor. I bought postcards from a twelve-year-old girl who will likely stop going to school because she can be more helpful to her family by making money from tourists than by getting an education. I've walked passed beggars lying on the side of the street who have been severely disfigured from the aftermath of Agent Orange in Vietnam. I've talked with young people in Myanmar who have to be very careful of what they say or do for fear of being imprisoned like many of their friends and family in the past.

I don't share these experiences to make anyone feel guilty or ashamed of the things we have in the United States. Rather, I give these examples of real hardships from around the world that most North Americans never face in their lifetime. According to a recent report from The World Factbook, U.S. citizens have a longer life expectancy than 182 other countries. In a 2014 report, the United States ranked tenth in the world in terms of freedom of choice, belief, expression, and economic mobility. Claiming that U.S. citizens have more privilege than other countries around the world may seem presumptuous or even arrogant, but when looking at the numbers related to basic human rights it's a hard truth—a privilege—that must be recognized.

Before my travels in Southeast Asia, I hardly thought about my national identity as a U.S. citizen. I was vaguely aware of global poverty, but had not really experienced it up close and in-person. Visiting country after country and seeing the same challenges around hunger, environmental degradation, and healthcare made me realize that I am incredibly fortunate, not because of what I've done but simply because of where I was born. While not everyone living in the countries I visited shares these troubling realities, traveling throughout Southeast Asia made my national identity and American privilege more salient than it ever was before.

Thinking more about national identity also got me thinking more complexly about national identity in other contexts, like back home in the United States. Aeriel's Asian identity is regularly used as a way to question her national identity in the States.

"Where are you from?" is one of the most asked questions she experiences living in the U.S.. My good friend who immigrated to California from Mexico at an early age has endured a lifetime of challenges, including constant threats of deportation and separation from her family. These were circumstances that I never experienced or even knew of throughout my life.

Interestingly enough, as my travels ended, my awareness of my national identity faded to the background. Being immersed back into the U.S., where the majority of people shared my same national identity, made nationality less important. In its place, gender and race took over as the identities that I've thought about the most. Identity salience is fluid and the lens through which we see the world changes all the time depending on where we are and who we're with.

PANING

AERIEL: In December of 2010, I attended a powerful social justice institute. This week-long immersion was a profound racial identity experience for me. As it turned out, Kyle, too, had attended the same conference previously. Within the first few minutes of introducing ourselves to one another, we realized that we shared this institute as a common experience. This connected us in a deep and meaningful way. As a part of the curriculum of the conference, both Kyle and I were introduced to an identity-awareness strategy called "PANing."

PAN is an acronym that stands for Pay Attention Now. The purpose of PANing is to practice a heightened level of awareness on how identity plays out in everyday life. To PAN, one must strive to be conscious of the way that identity influences and/or shows up in our interactions with others. For example, this could include noticing at the airport what perceived identities the travelers and/or pilots may have in comparison to the airport cleaning crew. A key element of PANing is the act of making an observation while withholding judgement. In thinking back on my college experience, I can PAN that all of my professors in my Strategic Communications major were people I perceived to be

White. Again, the point of PANing is to notice and name identity but to stop short of making any judgements or conclusions. Rather than postulating about the systemic barriers that lead to academia being a predominantly White space, PANing encourages me to reflect on what identity patterns I observe without crafting a story behind those dynamics.

In my own social justice journey, I have found PANing to be a useful tool to begin cultivating a more intentional and identity-aware mindset. In social justice consulting, I use the concept of PANing as an introductory tool to foster identity awareness. I think the skill of noticing identity dynamics is a critical step in being able to effectively work to dismantle systems of oppression. It's like the TSA public service announcement, "If you see something, say something." I have found it is difficult to encourage intervention without first developing the capacity for observation.

STEREOTYPES, ASSUMPTIONS, AND COLORBLINDNESS

AERIEL: Identity can be a very powerful and empowering concept in social justice journeying. However, there are also limitations and misperceptions regarding identity that we must acknowledge. For instance, since it is not commonplace for people to wear name badges with a comprehensive list of all of their social identities taped to their foreheads, others' identities may sometimes be unclear to us.

In fact, there may be times that because of the socialized nature of our communities, we make assumptions about others and put them into socially constructed boxes so we know how best to interact with them. This can be problematic in a number of ways. First, your perception of someone else's identity could be wrong. Second, many people don't like being put into boxes. So even if you presume someone's identity accurately, how you have come to understand this identity may drastically differ from how they experience that identity.

An example: I am Asian. I have dark brown hair, almond eyes, and a small nose. Phenotypically, others might quickly assume that I am of Asian descent. While this is not inaccurate, the limitation in this assumption is what others' extrapolate an Asian identity to mean. For instance, I am often asked if I speak the Korean language or if I am good at math. These questions are rooted in others' perceptions of my race and their association of Asianness with certain stereotypes and expectations.

Another example. While working at a college institution I had the privilege of getting to know a second-year student who identified as gender non-conforming. While this student was confident with their own gender identity and expression, their peers and even faculty and staff administrators had a difficult time grasping and accepting this student's identity. From an early age in the United States, we are socialized to adhere to a gender-binary: man and woman. When a mother is pregnant, one of the first questions strangers ask is "Is it a boy or a girl?"

This question reveals a fascinating tendency around identity—that once an identity is known or labeled, we as a society feel as though we have sufficient information to process and categorize a person accordingly. So, for my second-year student who identifies as gender non-conforming, others' inability to categorize them as a man or a woman led to confusion because they weren't able to access or rely upon the traditional notions of gender and thus felt at a loss for how to perceive and process the student.

This confusion led to embarrassment and insecurity and often resulted in others distancing themselves from the student. This is a sad, but real example of how important our assumptions and perceptions of others can be to our own sense of self. When the ability to perceive and thus socially place others is muted or challenged in any way—when someone doesn't fit into what we expect or our perception of who they are doesn't compute with how they see themselves—we become defensive. Our identity frame of reference is disrupted, and as a result, so is our own sense of self, which can be wholly unnerving.

A related, albeit distinctly different potential misperception with identity happens in the pursuit of social inclusion. Sometimes in an effort to foster a community of acceptance and equality, we seek to minimize difference. This, in the context of racial identity, is commonly referred to as "colorblindness." The limitation of colorblindness is not in the philosophical principle, but rather the practical application.

For example, my mother, like most parents, raised me in the belief that I should be treated the same as every other child in our neighborhood. This of course is an understandable and philosophically inclusive parental paradigm. I remember that as I was growing up, my mom would tell me that race shouldn't matter. She didn't want others to treat me different or less than because of the color of my skin or the shape of my eyes.

While this is a well-intended approach to race in regards to child rearing, the challenge for me was that my lived experience taught me otherwise. In actuality, I was treated differently, sometimes stared at and questioned if I was really my mother's daughter. Without intending to, an unfortunate byproduct of my mom's colorblind parenting was that it minimized my encounters with racism. This of course was the exact opposite of what she had hoped, which was to create a community where I would be included and treated the same as everyone else.

I remember one day in grade school, rushing home from the bus stop in tears. I ran into the warmth and safety of my mom's arms and confessed the hurtful things a bully at school had said to me. A girl in my class had publicly taunted me about my slanted eyes and oily hair and got the other kids to laugh and point at me. I can only imagine now as an adult, the heartbreak this must have meant for my mother.

Wiping the tears from my face and smoothing back my hair with kindness and love, my mom told me that the bully was stupid, mean, and insecure. She assured me that I was beautiful and reminded me that I needn't let the hurtful remarks of one person get me down. Her words could not have been more true. What she could not have known, however, was that this message had an unintended consequence. It treated my experience as an isolated encounter. Emphasizing one incident or ignorant person to overcome, rather than recognizing and preparing me to be resilient in light of a pattern of bias.

I know with the utmost certainty that my mother has always loved me with an unparalleled ferocity. She has never seen my Asianness as a detriment, distinguishing characteristic, or alien feature. As such, she has expected and hoped that others would see me and treat me equally and fairly. Unfortunately, the rest of the world does not work the same way. I was not the same as the other kids in my grade growing up. I did look different and I did have a different experience.

Colorblindness or equality is an ideal, one that is short sighted because it suggests that we treat everyone the same rather than recognize their differences. This means that we do not honor or acknowledge the unique lived experiences of people of color, the LGBTQ+ community, or people with disabilities. While I can understand the positive intentions behind colorblindness and equality, chiefly protection and harmony, I also know the potentially negative outcomes associated with those goals in our current society: silencing and minimization. In her brilliant TED Talk in 2014, businesswoman Mellody Hobson suggests a philosophical alternative to colorblindness; she challenges us to be "color brave."

This approach gets closer to the heart of where we need to be.

Color brave, as Ms. Hobson explains, is the notion that instead of shying away from conversations about race and identity, we lean in. When we don't acknowledge these aspects of who we are, we don't acknowledge whole parts of our lives and the lives of those around us. By choosing to be color brave we take the courageous path of talking about the taboo (race, gender, religion, etc.) in order to develop empathy, understanding, and inclusion of all identities.

VITAL Practice: Identity

Here are some concrete examples of how you can incorporate the second tenet of VITAL—Identity—into your daily life:

- Take five minutes to write down the full list of your identity categories. Start with the D7+ (race/ethnicity, gender, sexuality, religion/spirituality, socioeconomic class, ability status, and age). From there, go on to write out all of the different identities that are salient in your life. Whether its language and national origin or being a parent, seeing all of the different identity categories in front of you will help you visualize how much of your life is impacted by identity.

- Read a book about a social identity category that you do not often think about. Reading about the lived experiences of those with different identities from our own allows us to complicate our socialized understandings of those identities. The Social Justice Training Institute (www.sjti.org) has a wonderful bibliography of books that can help you get started.

- Attend an event hosted by a group with different identities from your own. From seeing a Native American Pow-Wow ceremony or attending a different religious service to celebrating the Lunar New Year or watching a play for the Deaf, going outside of our identity groups can allow us to see a new side of others' lived experiences.

CHAPTER 5:
TRUST

Everything will be okay in the end. If it's not okay, it is not yet the end.
—Unknown

When discussing how to effectively work across differences, trust is often the first value that comes up. Being able to trust the person across the table from you is extremely important and allows for strong teams to develop regardless of differences in personalities or identities.

Additionally, while we believe this type of face-to-face trust is essential, our emphasis on trust in the VITAL model has an added layer. When we talk about the importance of trust in social justice work, our focus is twofold: building trusting relationships and learning to trust the process.

Core to building trusting relationships is the creation of what we call *brave space*. Many social justice journeyers may have previously adhered to or worked within the construct of safe space; the establishment early on in group norming of a commitment to mutual respect. Brave space goes one step further. Rather than claiming to create a space where all participants will feel safe, which is virtually impossible to ensure, brave space focuses on the responsibility of individuals to gauge their own levels of comfort and determine how far outside of their comfort zones they are willing to go.

While we know that everyone has a different level of comfort when exploring issues related to identity and social justice, we also know that going outside of our comfort zones is where profound learning can happen. As author and leadership expert Robin Sharma said, "As you move outside of your comfort zone, what was once the unknown and frightening becomes your new normal."

The brave space approach says that we should all aim to be courageous in our social justice journey by first identifying where our comfort zone is and then pushing ourselves beyond that point to the extent that feels right for each of us. Brave space asks us to teeter in that area between our comfort zones and where we feel unsafe, right at the point of our learning edge. Whether developing trust between individuals in a group or learning to trust your own instincts when engaging in self-work, brave space can be a helpful tool in navigating those challenging moments that push us in our social justice journey.

Reflecting on one's own privileges and biases can be challenging. Experiencing true vulnerability—the kind of honest dialogue that causes the pit of your stomach to tighten and drop to the floor—is a jarring experience that most people avoid at all costs. Thinking critically about your own identities and how they have impacted your life can cause a flood of intense emotions, from frustration and fear to anxiety and hopelessness.

Despite these daunting realities the personal benefits of social justice work—including heightened self-awareness, healthier relationships, and clearer purpose—far outweigh the challenges of the process.

Trusting the process is sticking with it even when things are difficult, even when it's easier to default back to complacency as a means of self-preservation. Trusting the process is a conscious choosing of a different path, the path of sitting with the discomfort, knowing that not only will you survive but you will come out stronger on the other side. The challenge is to lean in to the discomfort, to the extent that is safe for you, trusting that the process will transform you and expand your learning edge.

LEANING INTO DISCOMFORT

KYLE: When Aeriel and I first met in 2011, we were traveling together in Cinque Terre, Italy. Over the course of three days, we ate delicious food, danced with locals at a rooftop party, and hiked across the breathtaking landscapes along the Mediterranean coast. We also shared stories and started to develop romantic feelings for each other.

Towards the end of the adventure, it became clear that we wanted to pursue something more serious. Knowing this, I decided that I had to be honest with Aeriel about my most recent relationship and how that might impact things moving forward. I knew it would be uncomfortable to tell Aeriel that I had just cut ties with someone I had been involved with for several years, but I believed she had a right to know.

As we boarded a ferry boat from Riomaggiore to Vernazza, I initiated the conversation and told her about this other person in my life. I was clear that there wasn't anything between us, but that I had just ended things a month before. I told Aeriel that spending this time with her in Italy made me realize what I had been missing in my previous relationship. The authentic appreciation and open communication we shared in just a few days had been a breath of fresh air and I hoped it could develop into something more.

She was grateful that I had been honest with her. In fact, it opened the door for her to do the same. Later in the conversation, she shared how meaningful it was to talk openly about race and social justice with me, whereas that had not always been a central part of her past relationships.

Despite the discomfort, this conversation allowed Aeriel and I to take our relationship to a deeper level. We each took a risk in sharing something vulnerable. Instead of dividing us, however, it brought us closer together. Our vulnerability with each other demonstrated a willingness to share and a willingness to be heard without judgement.

While it wasn't easy, I know that conversation transformed our relationship. We chose the difficult path of leaning into discomfort, trusting the process to guide us in the right direction. Not knowing which direction that would be was scary, but in the end it proved to be well worth the anxiety. Instead of scaring each other away, being vulnerable allowed us to establish an expectation of honesty in our relationship.

This is the power of trusting the process.

THE FIRST STEP

KYLE: While trusting yourself is foundational, trusting others is an essential part of moving forward on the social justice journey. Having trust in others can also be one of the most difficult things to do in practicing social justice.

In order to be vulnerable and openly share a personal story, an element of trust has to exist between individuals. Establishing that trust can be difficult, especially if there is a history of conflict or tension between the groups who are attempting to work across differences. Typically one person in the dialogue has to take the risk of being vulnerable first, and this opens the door for others to do the same.

This first act of open sharing can, often within minutes, transform the dynamic of a relationship from surface level to deep trust. It doesn't always happen right off the bat, but the first person to courageously offer a story they might not share widely or an opinion they might otherwise keep to themselves can alter the course of a relationship.

If trust has been established, that moment of vulnerability might be met with respect and empathy.

It may also be met with disagreement or conflict, but these are not indicators of distrust. In fact, the ability for individuals to engage in healthy conflict can be a great indicator of trust. These moments of discord remind us that someone can disagree with our words while simultaneously respecting us as people with valid lived experiences.

Determining who will take the first step of vulnerability in establishing trust between individuals can be a tricky proposition. Putting oneself on the line, whether it be an opinion or a personal story, can be scary when clear trust hasn't yet been developed. In any group setting, whether an important board meeting at the office or a family gathering during the holiday season, power dynamics likely come into play. Someone has seniority or has hosting power and someone is the neophyte or newbie. Regardless of the specific context, social power dynamics are a core consideration in cultivating a trusting and brave space. Multipartiality is an intentional effort to balance these power dynamics and equalize the space to foster trust.

An example of multipartiality was when Aeriel and I co-facilitated a seminar on race and racism with the staff and faculty of a predominantly White high school. Recognizing that I (given my Whiteness and maleness) would have credibility, power, and positionality from the get-go, we were intentional in crafting a facilitation agenda that featured Aeriel starting the day off. In this experience, multipartiality meant carving out intentional space for Aeriel to show up as the first facilitator voice and leader in order to challenge any power dynamics that may have otherwise favored my race and gender identities.

Multipartiality is a principle that outlines the delicate balance between vulnerability and co-optation. In other words, when people of different identities engage in difficult dialogue, there are times when those with more privilege should speak up and there are other times when people who experience more oppression should have space to share their perspectives. According to multipartiality, those with privilege should be the ones taking the risk in sharing vulnerability. Those who have marginalized identities should not have to take on the additional burden of being vulnerable before trust is established. In fact, there are times when it may not be safe for those people to do so. Multipartiality is a clear example of how those with dominant identities can leverage their privilege to help create positive change.

When Aeriel and I first started facilitating together, the principle of multipartiality helped us navigate the way our different identities surfaced in dialogue. By nature, my facilitation style was more friendly and jovial, whereas Aeriel tended to be more professional. I couldn't get over the differences in our style and would often critique her methods. After a few rough trainings where our styles conflicted, we finally sat down and talked about why we utilize such different styles.

In thinking about my identities—White, straight, cisgender male—Aeriel pointed out that it makes sense that I would have the confidence to crack jokes during facilitation. Given the privilege that I experience, I rarely have to worry about getting respect or being taken seriously by those that I work with. She, on the other hand, has had a lifetime of trying to prove herself and her facilitation style is a reflection of that experience. As a womyn of color, when Aeriel enters spaces, she often feels as though she has to earn respect, whereas I usually feel like I have it without doing anything at all. While both styles are equally effective in their own right, they are a clear representation of our identities at play.

Turning to the concept of multipartiality, we considered our identities and our facilitation styles when determining how to engage a group in dialogue. Given Aeriel's identities, we decided that it made more sense for her to lead the dialogue and be the first to speak. In a way, this would frame her as the leader and give her space and authority to utilize her voice. I would step in during moments where we needed to role model vulnerability for the group. For example, if we were asking the participants to share a time when they perpetuated discrimination, I would be the first to share a story. Given my privilege, it made more sense for me to take the risk of being vulnerable.

Multipartiality is a complex and tricky balance to strike. As someone with mostly dominant identities, my role in establishing trust is taking risk and sharing vulnerability. At the same time, I have to be mindful of the space that I take up in dialogue, being sure not to dominate the conversation and silence other voices. Conversely, Aeriel should be given space to share her perspective while not feeling like she is required to do so. The goals of multipartiality are lofty, but they offer clear representations for how to navigate risk and vulnerability when working to establish trust.

Another aspect of building trust between individuals is negotiating the difference between intent and impact. Someone may share an opinion or a story with the best of intentions but the impact of those words can end up offending or even hurting others.

For example, I may have a conversation with someone about safety when traveling in different countries around the world. In my efforts to help the other person practice caution, I might say something like, "You need to be careful in South Africa. Protect your valuables and don't even think about walking alone at night." Regardless of the truth of this statement, I've also made an implicit judgement about the country of South Africa and the people who live there. If someone from that country were to overhear my conversation, the impact of my words might be something different than a message of safety. That person might hear an American disrespecting their home and describing their people strictly as criminals or thieves.

As someone who benefits from tremendous privilege, I understand how blinding that privilege can be. It often makes me unaware of the impact of my words because I rarely have to think about what it might be like to be on the other side of them. Understanding the difference between intent and impact allows me to see how my privilege, without intentionally trying to wield it, can negatively affect others.

There are two important aspects of developing this type of trust. They are:

- Assuming the best intent, and

- Apologizing when the impact is harmful.

An important condition of navigating intent versus impact is not to censor what we say, but rather to accept responsibility for both our intentions and the impact of our words. While the impact of people's words might be negative, it's crucial to keep in mind that their intentions were likely positive and well-meaning. Very seldom in social justice dialogue does someone blatantly say or do something with the intention of hurting others. However, even those with the best of intentions can say things that hurt or offend others simply due to the limitations of their own world view.

Assuming good intent and apologizing when our impact is harmful can allow us to maintain perspective during conflict. It reminds us that the person across the table is trying their best. It also reminds us to be humble and own our actions even if they have unintended consequences. This give and take of expectations and responsibility enables us to gracefully engage in dialogue with empathy and compassion. Trying to see from the other person's perspective will help clarify our own stance, and can allow for more honesty and trust when expressing how the words of another made us feel. This can be difficult to practice in the real world, considering how triggering some well-intended comments can be and given how frustrating it is to offend someone else when you're trying so hard not to. Despite these challenges, stepping back, taking a breath and thinking intentionally about intent vs. impact dynamics can be a significant step toward creating trust between individuals.

Knowing that you can folly, make a misstep, or tap out due to sheer exhaustion without judgment or criticism from your community is critical to staying engaged. Assuming good intent implies that we trust one another's intentions. This perspective provides the compassion necessary to look beyond a triggering comment. Instead of jumping to correct someone, assuming good intent shows up as a compassionate inquiry to better understand a different perspective. Instead of shutting down or zoning out, assuming good intent seeks to mindfully engage, understand and be in a relationship with one another as we work towards our common goal.

Trust the Process

AERIEL: It wasn't until graduate school that I encountered the concept and phrase, "trust the process." During the spring of my senior year in college I attended a preview weekend event where faculty and current students offered advice to prospective students in the master's program. Early on in the Q&A session, a potential new student asked what it was like working so closely with 14 other peers, given the program's cohort model. One of the panelists responded, "It can be a lot: taking all of your classes together, working on group projects together, often times living together, sometimes dating one another . . . but trust the process, it all works out."

A handful of current students who were dispersed around the room lightly chuckled.

Another prospective student sitting in the audience raised his hand a little while later and asked how one figures out if he should do a seminar paper and pursue a M.Ed. or if he should go the thesis route and aim for an M.A. This time an esteemed faculty member responded, saying, "It depends on the individual student. You don't need to know right now. Trust the process. Through coursework, conversations with your advisor, and as you gain clarity about what you hope to do after finishing the program, you'll make the right decision for you."

For me, as a type-A planner, sitting in this large classroom in the basement of the education building on a campus I had never visited prior, next to people I didn't know, and miles away from friends and family... the ambiguity of the phrase "trust the process" was vague, unnerving, and did not feel helpful.

How was I supposed to trust the process if I didn't understand what the process entailed or even really know the people I was going to experience the process with?

Fast forward about a year and again I found myself in the same large classroom in the basement of the education building for an event during preview weekend, but this time I was answering the questions. When asked to share about my experience, I spoke about coursework, learning from both the faculty and the peers in my cohort, and, yes, the importance of "trusting the process."

As I said those three words, the irony of my circumstance and that I was dispensing the same vague advice I had felt frustrated by just one year previous caused me to laugh out loud. Upon composing myself, I went on to explain that the philosophy of trusting the process is really about valuing the experience of discovery as much as the end outcome which you're striving toward.

In graduate school, many things happen beyond a linear course progression towards a degree. Sure, a common reason many people pursue graduate school is to obtain another credential. However, the learning and transformation that happens in a graduate program is much more vast, complex, challenging, and rewarding than simply what is reflected in a class syllabus. You have high highs (like collaborating with an admired faculty mentor on a stimulating research project) and you have low lows (like feeling overwhelmed or discouraged as you learn about systems of power, privilege, and oppression). But the experience isn't limited to any of these moments in isolation; the reward comes from stepping back and appreciating the process in its entirety.

CLEANING HOUSE

AERIEL: "It always gets worse before it gets better!" Mom would declare whenever we worked to clean her office or our home. And somehow this was always the case.

Rather than lightly dusting whatever surfaces were exposed, we'd end up taking everything off every shelf and making huge piles throughout the living room then crawled around like it was an obstacle course. Things would start off looking a little disorganized, but manageable, and within an hour of "tidying up," the office would look like a paper monster threw up all over the place. Receipts, old notebooks, and samples of her writing lay strewn about all over the floor. For Mom, trusting the process was integral to her approach to housework. She didn't singularly fixate on the outcome of a spotless shiny office or living room and then take the most efficient route to that end. Rather, she immersed herself in the process of organizing and cleaning, taking extra time and care to look through old receipts and flip through books that had otherwise been gathering dust.

Cleaning house with Mom was not just a necessary chore, it was a reflective process. Though this wasn't my preferred style of cleaning, I did learn an important lesson from her: that sometimes it gets messier before it gets better. I think this lesson rings true for social justice journeying as well.

Offering up pieces of yourself, your story, and your lived experience is a precious thing, and needs to be regarded as such. The privilege of bearing witness to another's social justice journey is truly a gift. Though our work may feel messy, every part of it should be handled with great care.

TRUST YOURSELF

AERIEL: Facing the world's injustices head on and alone can be daunting and wholly overwhelming. That's why relationship, fellowship, and community are so important. Creating infrastructures of support are essential and enable us to lean on one another and better sustain each other for the long journey. Trust is the centerpiece of these relationships.

Another important layer of trust is the ability to trust oneself. Often when engaging in these highly emotive dialogues around issues of identity, diversity, and social justice it can seem like there's a right and a wrong way to "show up." This couldn't be further from the truth. In fact, when we succumb to insecurities and begin to self-censor, we disrupt the entire process. Trusting ourselves, our instincts, our persistent questions, and our heart's intentions is necessary to being vulnerable and showing up authentically. The moment we begin to hold back and doubt the value of our contributions is the moment the group's relational trust begins to falter.

Now of course this doesn't mean we should go blazing into every conversation spouting our convictions or beliefs as the one and only truth. But it does mean we need to trust our inner voices and be equitable in sharing and creating learning and journeying spaces—even if that means making mistakes or possibly offending someone. Creating relationships and community is based on trust; it requires both the strength and the willingness to be vulnerable. The moment individuals begin to self-censor is the moment group cohesion and trust begins to suffer. Trusting yourself doesn't come from a place of arrogance, it is rooted in humility. It demands offering up your perspective, ideas, and curiosity while welcoming the lived experiences and narratives of others.

White Woman's Tears

AERIEL: I remember a specific instance when one of my fellow social justice journeyers, a self-identified White woman, broke down into tears. Overwhelmed by the stories shared and the magnitude of racial injustice, her stress, guilt, and frustration poured through in her tears.

I share this story for two reasons. First, to demonstrate the importance of trusting relationships. In her moment of emotion, I knew that I had to trust her and assume positive intent if we were going to effectively continue our social justice journeying together. If I doubted her sincerity or questioned her authenticity, my withdrawal and/or vocal criticism would have impeded our group's ability to delve deeper. So in assuming positive intent, I was able to put my ego aside, and approach this fellow participant from a place of compassion. I recognized her tears as an outpour of complex emotions rather than a reposition of attention on the needs of her as a White woman. Additionally, I had to trust myself and my gut, which compelled me to articulate to the group that seeing her as a White woman cry in light of racial injustice was difficult because I didn't feel I had the emotional, mental, or physical capacity to comfort her in her pain.

My ability to trust myself and show up authentically by naming my reaction to her emotions was intimidating because I did not want to come across as the heartless womyn of color. In the end, our trust allowed the group to delve deeper, to unpack the roots of the White woman's tears and to ultimately challenge the unspoken societal expectation that people of color should soothe her feelings of guilt. In this story, trusting the process was integral to the group and trusting each other allowed the group to make meaning of the exchange in a powerful way.

VITAL PRACTICE: TRUST

Here are some concrete examples of how you can incorporate the third tenet of VITAL—Trust—into your daily life:

- Write out a list of three times in which you succeeded on your social justice journey and three times in which you fell short. Review the list of successes and think of the steps you took along the way that helped you achieve your goal. Next, review the list of failures and think of what you learned as a result of not hitting the target. Routinely evaluating your actions and how they contribute to a larger picture will help you gain perspective and appreciation for the process.

- Meditate, practice yoga, or go for a walk if you are able. In all of these exercises, you are required to focus on the process as well as the outcome. When meditating, the goal is simply to clear your mind and the only way to do that is to engage in the process of mindful breathing. When walking, the aim may be to arrive at a destination, but the journey requires action. Be reflective about each step and consider how they are valuably independent from your ultimate arrival.

- Make a commitment and keep it. Practicing follow-through in social justice journeying helps us develop our capacity to trust the process. Whether finding ways to consistently demonstrate your commitment to gender inclusion by using preferred gender pronouns in introductions or finishing a book on social justice journeying, commit to your goals by engaging in the process.

CHAPTER 6: AUTHORSHIP

One of the most valuable things we can do to heal one another is to listen to each other's stories.
—Rebecca Falls

Personal stories are one of the most powerful tools in social justice work. The simple act of telling your story and bearing witness to someone else's lived experience can build incredible bridges across differences because it requires both parties to be vulnerable and listen without judgement.

Sharing your story takes courage. You can never be sure how someone will respond once you tell them your story. This is why most of us have just a few very close friends who are privy to the intimate details of our lives. Like the trapeze artist standing at the edge of the platform, revealing your personal truth can be like taking a leap of faith. If all goes well, you will find not open air but open hands, an experience that will deepen your connection.

Listening to someone share their story is a gift both for the person sharing and for the person listening because it requires full attention and humility. Instead of merely waiting for your turn to talk, active listening requires you to suspend your inner monologue and fully immerse yourself in what the other person is saying. This type of attention during conversation is rare, which also highlights why many of us don't feel comfortable vulnerably sharing our stories. When the person across the table actually demonstrates that they will humbly and fully bear witness to your truth, sharing your story becomes a welcome opportunity to be authentically heard.

Most importantly, stories have the power to develop empathy in a way that discussions and debates about facts cannot. It is difficult to argue with the way that someone feels. The naysayer cannot refute an actual lived experience. Stories, unlike arguments or rhetoric, have the unique ability to transform our view of the world through the head and the heart. When we hear someone's story, we discover their unique truth and also realize commonalities that we may have never otherwise considered.

OUR STORY

AERIEL: Rooted in our belief that authorship and the art of storysharing are important tools for social justice journeying, we thought it important to share a bit of our own story and how we came to be so passionate about this work.

We met in the summer of 2011 at an international higher education conference. From our very first conversation, we felt a sparked connection. Both of us identified as children of divorce and were raised by strong single mothers. While Kyle was the youngest of three boys and I was an only child, our shared admiration for our mothers was apparent in our respective narratives and created an immediate bond between us.

We had also both previously experienced transformative shared social justice training in our professional journeys. This prior experience was meaningful for both of us and left a lasting impression. When we realized we had this unique learning experience in common, we found comfort, familiarity, and excitement in a shared language around issues of identity, diversity, and equity.

For Kyle and I, the cliché, "timing is everything," couldn't have been more true. We often reflect on how important our meeting at that specific time in each of our lives was to our connection. I had recently gotten out of a two-and-a-half-year relationship. In addition to wanting different things, my boyfriend and I ultimately decided to go our separate ways because while he appreciated my passion for racial justice, he also found it overwhelming. I acutely remember in one of our many pre-breakup conversations, him telling me that my critical justice lens was "just too much."

Heartbroken and deflated, I struggled for a few months after we separated with how to reconcile and prioritize my romantic life and my social justice journey. Ultimately, I determined that I could not compromise on my commitment to issues of racial justice and that I was not able or willing to tone down my critical race lens. Resolved to spend the rest of my years a passionate social justice journeyer—even if that meant I would be single with seven cats—I at least felt conviction in my clarity of values.

At the time we met, Kyle, too, was recovering from romantic uncertainty. Having been immersed in an on-again off-again long-distance unrequited love for over a year, he was unsure of new romance. But being a tender heart his whole life, he found resiliency and hope in our shared openness and communication, not only about our professional passions and values, but also about our romantic feelings for one another.

Like any good fairy tale romance, our meeting is full of clichés. "When you know, you know."

While both Kyle and I had been on independent journeys romantically and in terms of our social justice values, when we met it was apparent within a few days that we had stumbled across a very special bond. Within a few months of our meeting in Switzerland, we decided to embark on an adventure of love and exploration together.

The years that followed have been a whirlwind of great love, incredible travel, and deepening our social justice learning with one another. Not only are we able to process our triggers and author our stories with one another, but the foundation of our partnership is built upon a strong and growing passion for the work. Over breakfast, while driving to the grocery store, and even before falling asleep, we regularly reflect on how dynamics of power and privilege surface in our everyday life. We discuss thoughtfully and vulnerably our social justice values in the context of current events and important relationships in our lives. We share stories and realizations about the interplay of our identities and lived experiences as we seek to lean into our learning edges and support one another as we step outside of our comfort zones and into brave spaces.

For years we have been facilitating social justice workshops as well as speaking and teaching on issues of racial justice and gender equity. We have grown our marriage in and of these values and continue to center our relationship around our individual and collective social justice journeying.

Over the past few years we have begun to notice patterns in our social justice journey and in the stories of others who are journeying too. One of the most pressing and common trends is a desire for community.

Kyle and I are fortunate to have a built-in processor, listener, and accountability partner in our marriage. However, as we've done speaking engagements and workshop facilitations with others who are on a social justice journey, it has become apparent that not everyone has access to this same sort of community. We share our example of marriage to demonstrate the power of authorship and finding community in sharing your social justice journey with others.

SIPPING HOT CHOCOLATE

KYLE: Imagine yourself winding through the Swiss Alps onboard a high-speed train. You are traveling from the Italian region in Switzerland to the towering mountain village of Visp, near Zermatt. As the train pulls into a layover station, you grab your bags full of heavy winter gear for skiing, and lumber your way off the train. The stop is at the border of Italy and Switzerland, a small pass-through in order to avoid the tallest heights of the Alps en route.

You find your way to your assigned seat on the connecting train and pull out your thermos full of piping hot chocolate. Sipping the sweet beverage, you observe other passengers making their way onboard. You notice that there are a few passengers boarding who speak languages other than Italian and you wonder where they might be coming from.

As the passengers settle into their seats, the car doors open with a rush of chilly alpine air and two border control officers announce themselves. The entire train car goes silent and you reach for your passport in case they ask for documentation. Leading the two officers is a ferocious looking German shepherd, sniffing each row of seats from one end of the car to the other.

As the officers scan the passengers, they focus their gaze on the row of seats just ahead of you and to the left. A dark-skinned woman wearing a head covering is sitting there trying to quiet her two children. She is speaking a language that sounds entirely foreign to your untrained ears. The officers pass by everyone on the train and make a direct line to the woman and her children.

Soon the officers and the family are engaging in a heated exchange. The woman produces all of the requested documentation, including train tickets and passports, but the officers are not satisfied. The questioning persists for several minutes until finally they command the family off the train. The other passengers in the train car seem unfazed by the altercation, but you are baffled by the blatant profiling you just witnessed. No one else onboard was even asked for their paperwork, but the one family of color was questioned with hostility and then promptly removed from the train.

As you slowly pull away from the station, you watch the mother and her children fade off into the distance through your window. Wherever they were hoping to go, you realize that they won't be getting there on time. You also wonder how many of these unscheduled detainments that same family has experienced while traveling in Europe. *Have I ever been stopped or aggressively questioned by border officials or by anyone for that matter?* you ask yourself.

For me, the answer to this question is *no*. Not once have I ever been questioned on a train.

It's a true story. I actually rode the train through the Alps, sipped the hot chocolate, and witnessed the family being singled out by the Italian border patrol. While I couldn't follow much of the conversation, I want to believe the authorities had their justifications for the interrogation. Still, from my perspective, it seemed like blatant racial profiling. I'd heard that incidents like this were common in Europe, but it was shocking to see it done so overtly. Equally shocking was how little the other White passengers seemed to care.

I share this anecdote to illustrate a powerful point about storytelling and authorship. Unlike facts or opinions, stories are rooted in personal experience. Regardless of anyone's beliefs about racial profiling in Europe, I have a story that speaks to real people at a real time and place.

Instead of painting a word picture and asking you, the reader, to put yourself in the situation, I could have simply made a statement like, "Racial profiling is a problem in Europe." Both approaches make a similar point, but the way they get there is vastly different.

In a story, you hear the sounds, smell the smells, and see the sights. Stories frame characters who have feelings and emotions. Simply stating a fact about racial profiling in Europe doesn't put a face to the mother with her two children. It also doesn't illustrate them standing on the platform in the train station and freezing in the chilly alpine air. A story allows you to feel how someone in that situation felt, a form of empathy that can easily be avoided when only discussing facts and figures.

Don't get me wrong; I'm not encouraging people to ignore statistics or factual evidence. But I don't think they are powerful tools on their own for developing the empathy and compassion our social justice journeying so desperately demands. Woven together to create a story, numbers and figures can be incredibly moving, but many statisticians will attest to the insignificance of a single point of data. The real power is the stories that can be told with that data.

When engaging in social justice work, authorship through storysharing is crucial in working effectively across differences. Given the complexity of the issues at hand, including racism, gay rights, and gender equity to name a few, it is tempting to fall into debates about numbers or theoretical philosophizing about hypothetical scenarios. The most effective approach, however, is to engage in meaningful dialogue that focuses on personal lived experiences and real stories.

EMPOWERMENT

KYLE: When we are given the opportunity to author our own stories and feel safe enough to share them, we are empowered. Having time and space to use one's voice can be a rare occasion for many. Whether in the form of what we see in movies, the headlines we read in the newspapers or the 30-second sound clip we hear on the radio, we typically see and hear a single perspective. The frenetic pace of American culture seldom leaves time for anything but a dualistic black or white picture of any issue. Meaningful and effective social justice work involves relationships, groups, and organizations that value authorship as a means to unpacking the multiple complex stories that we all bring to the table. In other words, it places immense importance on the grey.

Allowing members of a group to author their own stories can be extremely time consuming, but the investment is well worth the end result.

Several years ago, I was the director of a college orientation program. For many who have attended university for the first time, you might well remember being ushered around the first few days on campus by an overly enthusiastic orientation leader who seemingly knew all the answers to your endless questions and had a wardrobe full of brightly-colored neon clothing. In my role, I was responsible for organizing the orientation program as well as training the student orientation leaders who would welcome the new students to our school.

The orientation leaders, arriving about a week before orientation was set to begin, were a ragtag team of energetic students who couldn't wait to lead their first campus tour. Before being given their T-shirt and clipboard, however, they needed a bit of training to ensure they would be ready for the task at hand. I knew that the week of orientation would be challenging and the team would have to trust and rely on each other for help. This meant we had to spend some time building relationships and getting to know one another.

One of the first exercises I facilitated to establish this group bond was called lifelines. Each night of training, after all of the preparation tasks were completed, we would gather around as a group and share our life stories. The instructions for the activity were simple. There were no time limits or restrictions, just an opportunity to share and have others listen.

For those not speaking, it was strictly a time to listen attentively and honor the story being shared.

The lifelines exercise with a group of eighteen people took about a week to complete. We would get through approximately three or four stories per night and each person would speak for at least forty-five minutes. Sometimes we would push through and stay up all hours of the night just to hear one more story. Tears were shed, secrets were revealed, and stomachs ached from laughter. It was time-consuming and exhausting, but it became by far everyone's favorite part of training.

Years later, I still have students reach out and tell me what a profound and life-changing experience the lifelines exercise was for them. Many had never intentionally set aside time to share their life story or listen to the stories of others. Doing this forced them to reflect on their lives in ways they hadn't, be vulnerable in ways that they wouldn't, and see the world from someone else's perspective in ways they couldn't.

In the end, the group bonded like I'd never seen before. They were like family after just one week. Many of them shared parts of their lives that even their best friends back home never knew. They had taken risks in being vulnerable about their personal histories and that vulnerability was received with respect and compassion. They trusted each other and they genuinely cared for each other.

In addition to establishing a strong team, the lifelines activity also allowed the students to have ownership over their experience. The opportunity and safe space to openly author their story enabled them to feel more confident and in control of their experience. They weren't just student workers completing tasks for orientation, they were individuals working together to create a meaningful experience for their fellow incoming classmates. They cared about their work in a way that they might not have if they hadn't been given the time and space to share their stories. They also cared about each other in a way that they might not have if they hadn't taken the time to listen to each other share their lifelines.

Each year the lifelines exercise became more and more popular among the orientation leader teams. Students would talk about the activity throughout the rest of the school year like legends being told over a campfire. Although I don't work at that school any more, I am told by students who still attend that some form of the lifelines exercise still happens during their trainings.

I share this story as an example of the power of authorship. Sharing stories and bearing witness to someone else's lived experiences are incredibly transformative practices. When we have the opportunity to author our own perspectives, we feel empowered to take ownership and show compassion towards others. When we intentionally listen to others' stories, our stereotypes begin to fade as we see ourselves in their lives.

Authorship might be the most effective and powerful tool in working toward social justice.

TRUTH-TELLING

AERIEL: Central to authorship is *storysharing*. By storysharing we mean an authentic and vulnerable exchange of lived experiences. We also call this truth-telling. In the many years that Kyle and I have facilitated social justice education, we have found stories to be one of the most effective approaches to engaging and deepening individuals' in their social justice practice. In the context of VITAL, stories are different from fairy tales and urban legends. Stories are first-person narratives that represent an individual's truth and real-life experiences.

What is so powerful about storysharing is that these stories cannot be refuted. Often people default to arguing statistics, presenting academic articles, and engaging in other forms of intellectual debate when trying to make a case for inclusion and diversity. While these approaches have a time and place, we have also found that they regularly spiral into a tit-for-tat debacle rather than lead to a productive and growing conversation. Stories on the other hand, when individuals are empowered to self-author and share their lived experience, cannot be so easily trivialized and disregarded. For instance, bearing witness to someone's story of being bullied in high school for her perceived sexual orientation builds empathy and coalitions in VITAL journeying much more than reading a research article about the statistics of queer harassment in education.

Authorship, the process of owning, writing, and sharing one's own story can be hugely liberating. Since the beginning of time, history has been documented by the few—the historically powerful and privileged majorities. Tragically, this has meant that generations of voices have been silenced and entire community narratives excluded. Authorship in the context of VITAL calls for the collection and presentation of these otherwise untold perspectives. Authorship calls into question that which we may have been told and sold (hegemonic single-voice stories) and invites those who have been marginalized to speak their truths.

In her TED Talk, *Danger of a Single Story*, Chimamanda Ngozi Adichie discusses the misunderstanding and disempowerment that can happen when our stories are authored by someone else. Growing up in Nigeria and studying in the United States, she experienced firsthand the power of the story that the Western world has written about

Africa, chiefly that it's a monolithic place. Her college roommate was astonished that she spoke English and assumed that she either came from a place of extreme poverty, violent genocide, or both. If all we knew of Africa was what we see in the Western media, we would only think of a place with breathtaking landscapes, starving children, and senseless wars resulting in death and destruction.

Unlike Africa, the United States has the privilege of writing many different stories for itself. Controlling major media outlets, the world has come to understand America as a complex place with people that range in abilities, emotions, and achievements. Conversely, American media outlets tend to only tell one type of story about the entire continent of Africa, and it is the one that Adichie's roommate expected when they first met. The impact of this single narrative is alarmingly dangerous, not only in the way that the rest of the world interacts with people from Africa, but also in the way that people from African nations may internalize some of these global expectations.

But thanks to writers like Chimamanda Ngozi Adichie, our understanding of Africa is more complex. She has dedicated her career to writing stories that complicate the dominant narrative of

Africa as a poverty-stricken warzone, painting scenes of joy and celebration of culture and creativity. These stories have inspired her fellow Nigerians and other Africans to feel empowered to tell their own stories, stories that humanize their people and their countries. Her words and her work remind us that when we author our own stories, we have the ability to take ownership of those stories and determine how they will end.

Rather than being told how and why one is the way they are, authorship empowers the individual by asserting that they know their experience best. Creating one's own narrative leads to ownership and connectedness, an investment that is invaluable when facilitating social justice movements.

MY ADOPTION STORY

AERIEL: I have never had a birth story—the family folklore that's told and retold every year on or around your birthday. I didn't grow up hearing how many hours were suffered in labor or what funny food combinations were craved during pregnancy. As an adoptee, these stories were never a part of my childhood. I did, however, have an adoption story. This was the story my mom told me about how I went from being born in Seoul, South Korea to being raised in Minnesota, USA.

The story I was told was that my biological parents met while in college. They were young, well-educated, and while they cared for one another, they quarreled often. At some point, this resulted in their breaking up, after which my biological mom found out that she was pregnant. It was (and still is today) very difficult to be an unwed mother in Korea. In fact, I recall being told that having a child out of wedlock would not only be disgraceful for my biological mother, but also that there would be a notation on all of my identification for the rest of my life, indicating that I was a bastard child. Thus, to avoid this cultural and public shaming, I was given up for adoption. According to my adoption story, my biological mother kept me as a secret, even from my biological father, and carried the weight of the pregnancy and adoption plan on her own.

As one might imagine, this adoption story impacted me deeply. Growing up, I was very dedicated to my studies and I attribute part of my career discernment in higher education to the fact that college was one of the only pieces of information I ever knew about my biological parents. Additionally, given what I was told about my biological mother dealing with the pregnancy on her own, I assumed my biological father did not know about me and perhaps didn't even know that he had fathered a child. Lastly, while shame was and still is a very real aspect of children born out of wedlock in Korea, as a young person, I had difficulty separating social norms and personal implications. Relatedly, I have often found myself sensitive to the colloquial use of the word "bastard," and for many years worried that there was a negative stigma related to my adoption.

In the summer of 2015, I traveled to Korea for the first time since I left as an infant 30 years prior.

On this emotional journey to my birth country, I learned more about my adoption story, including some new elements of my birth story. During a file review at my adoption agency, I found out that I was born at 7:15 A.M. on April 15, 1985. I also found out that my biological father was present for my birth. This experience as an adult has empowered me to take hold of and self-author my adoption story. There is still much I do not know, but since claiming my own narrative and framing my adoption through my own lens, I've found resiliency, strength, and pride.

BEARING WITNESS

AERIEL: Authorship's other half is less talked about but no less important: the art of listening. Stories lead to empathy in a way that can often result in strong alliances, which can be cultivated into social change coalitions. Additionally, in the practice of bearing witness to another's truth, we sometimes have new epiphanies about our own identities, lived experiences, prejudices, and social justice journeys. The practice of active listening—of making connections between the stories others are sharing and real experiences from one's own life—is important to effectively engage in social justice and VITAL practice.

Here's an example: Previously, while working at a university on the East Coast, I served as a facilitator for an intra-Asian dialogue. The goal of the dialogue was to explore the diverse lived experiences within the Asian community. Over the course of a semester, our small but mighty dialogue group sat together in a small circle talking about our experiences as Asian Americans and exploring the intersections of race, gender, socioeconomic class, and religion.

This dialogue was my first exposure to a Pan-Asian storysharing space rooted in social justice. It was profound and revealing. The stories my fellow dialogue participants shared about being the target of perpetual foreigner stereotypes and other racialized microaggressions was simultaneously heartbreaking and affirming. It was like they could read my mind, each person telling stories that I similarly had experienced at some point in my life. Bearing witness to other Asian Americans' truths was validating as I saw similarities in my own experience.

To know that I wasn't alone in my encounters with the ugly beast of racism was a relief. It wasn't until this dialogue that I was able to readily access self-determined Asian American narratives. The opportunity to author our own stories, rather than be expected to live up to model minority stereotypes was profoundly freeing. But sharing my voice was not only liberating, it was exhilarating. It allowed me to walk out into the world with a greater sense of self-awareness, supported by a community of others who had similar experiences.

This is the power of authorship.

VITAL PRACTICE: AUTHORSHIP

Here are some concrete examples of how you can incorporate the fourth tenet of VITAL—Authorship—into your daily life:

- Jot down critical incidents of your own social justice story. The paths of our social justice journeying may seem obvious to us, but rarely do we take the time to intentionally reflect upon and share them with others. Taking the time to do this can be profoundly illuminating. The act of authoring your own social justice story is a way to take ownership of your journey in a way that can be incredibly profound.

- Tell your story to someone you trust. It might seem scary, saying out loud the words of your story that you wrote on paper, but it can be a liberating and healing exercise. It is not often that someone will take the time to just sit and listen attentively to you tell your story, but there are likely a few people in your life who would if you asked. When you're done, ask them to reflect back to you what they heard and what resonated with them most. You may be surprised by the positive things you hear.

- Listen to someone share their story. Bearing witness to someone else's story is a gift. It allows that person to author their own truth and it allows you to hear a perspective that you might not have otherwise. Find someone you trust and ask them to tell you their story. If they're willing, make sure to reflect back to them the parts of their story that resonate with you the most.

CHAPTER 7: LIBERATION

Please use your liberty to promote ours.
—Aung San Suu Kyi

Liberation comes at the end of our VITAL model, and as such it truly does summarize all of the components we've already described. Through vulnerability, talking about identity, trusting the process, and practicing authorship, social justice journeyers are working to liberate themselves from the oppressive systems that negatively impact us all. While these are only a few of the pieces of a larger social justice puzzle, liberation through self-work is a crucial element to dismantling larger systemic structures of bias and discrimination.

Broadly speaking, liberation is about personal growth, healing, and social change. When we choose to do our own self-work around unearned power and privilege, we are setting in motion the wheels of transformation on every level. When we begin to unlearn the destructive messages we've been told that undervalue and disregard our marginalized identities, we are starting to heal a lifetime of oppressive wounds. Often, liberation requires us to evaluate our intersecting multiple identities by both evaluating certain aspects of privilege that we have as well as allowing us to heal from internalized oppression associated with our other identities.

Most importantly, liberation through personal development means aligning beliefs with actions. Saying that you are committed to social justice is one thing, but taking a hard look at everything you think, say, and do from the lens of that commitment is another thing entirely.

Liberation is a chance for us to create positive social change in the place where we have the most influence: ourselves. Indeed, it may be the most important and necessary place for liberation to happen exactly because we all have the ability to change any time we want. We simply have to decide that we want to start making the world a more equitable place and begin with ourselves.

As you've come to learn, the practice of liberation and self-work has the potential to go far beyond the individual level. When many individuals set out to create a change within themselves, it results in a critical mass of people working toward social justice.

As Aristotle wrote, "the whole is greater than the sum of its parts."

A group of likeminded individuals is a community, and communities have the potential to influence large-scale social change. From role modeling inclusive behavior and holding each other accountable to collective activism and influencing public policy, a group of individuals striving to improve themselves will inevitably have the potential to improve others.

From one-on-one conversations to large-scale social reform, all forms of social justice work are important and necessary. If the people doing that work haven't invested in a practice of liberation and self-work, however, that work has the potential to become inconsistent with social justice values. A sustained engagement in personal growth means a consistent analysis of one's own identities and the impact they have on those around them. It also involves continuously striving to understand the perspectives of those with different identities and lived experiences. Liberating oneself is an ongoing process that benefits all aspects of social justice work, starting from the ground up.

VALUING THE PROCESS

KYLE: In the spring of 2014, Aeriel and I were in the thick of packing up our lives before a cross-country move. We had been working at a college in New Hampshire for nearly two years and had decided the time was right for us to be closer to friends and family. With strong roots in the Midwest, we both felt somewhat displaced in the direct no-nonsense culture of the Northeast. We had been dreaming of branching off to start our own business and the move would provide a supportive network of friends and family that could help us get on our feet. With all of our belongings strategically Tetris-packed into a shipping cube, we turned our attention to spending one last weekend with the friends we had made in New Hampshire.

Our plan was to make the three-hour drive up to Montreal to enjoy the delicious food and soak up the energy in one of our favorite Canadian cities. Just minutes after the shipping cube was loaded onto the truck and carried away, we realized that in the haste of our frenzied packing we had forgotten to set aside our passports for the trip! Stored away in a small box inside the cube, our passports were now safely on their way to Saint Paul, Minnesota and we had no way of legally crossing the Canadian border.

We were crushed. Our hotel had already been booked and paid for and breaking the news to our friends was even more devastating. Our two closest friends in New Hampshire had been waiting to go to Montreal with us since we had been raving about our trip there a year earlier. Having done some adventurous traveling together already, we had grown accustomed to calling ourselves by the nickname of Team Transplant, referring to the serendipitous nature of how our transient lives brought us together. Canceling this, our last adventure together, was heartbreaking for us all.

As a last chance Hail Mary, one of our friends phoned her parents in Burlington, Vermont, to see if we might be able to alter our plans and instead stay at their place for the weekend. Burlington was one of the more vibrant cities in the area and it had become somewhat of a metropolitan escape for the four of us living in the secluded New Hampshire countryside. In many ways, it was probably more appropriate for us to have our final send-off there as opposed to a place where the four of us had never spent any time together. It just so happened that her parents were going to be out of town and were more than happy to let us watch the house while they were away.

It turned out that Burlington was the perfect place to spend our last weekend in the Northeast with our dearest friends. We walked the beautiful coast of Lake Champlain, sampled beverages at some of the nation's best breweries, and ate at our favorite taqueria one last time. Still, there was something missing.

Our friendship had been built on a sense of adventure and spontaneity that often seems to come when young professionals come together with little to capture their imaginations aside from the local TJ Maxx and a dingy movie theater known as the "sleazy-six" cinemas. One time we all jumped into a car on a whim and drove down to Miami where we hopped a ride on a four-day Caribbean cruise. Yet another time, we escaped to Providence, Rhode Island to stay at a bed and breakfast with a stripper pole built into the middle of the living room. Needless to say, our quiet final weekend in Burlington would not be complete without a little adventure!

We had been throwing around the idea of getting a group tattoo for a while, and we decided this was the perfect opportunity to make it happen. All of us were at a turning point in life, moving off in different directions, and memorializing our time together in permanent ink would be a fitting way to close this chapter of our lives and begin the next. We discussed and brainstormed at length all of the different tattoo possibilities during the entire two-hour drive up to Burlington. By the end of the first day we had definitively decided that we would get inked, but we weren't exactly sure what our group tattoo would be.

We woke the next morning sobered by the reality of what we were about to do. Up to that point we had discussed the idea of a single tattoo that we would all get—something symbolic of our friendship together. The best we could come up with was a hilarious image of a bunny rabbit wearing a winter ski cap that had become somewhat of a mascot for our group. Knowing that this would be on our bodies for the rest of our lives, we decided against the funny bunny and chose instead to all get individual tattoos that carried personal significance. The memory of us all getting tattoos on our last weekend together, we decided, was momentous enough.

I had been toying with the idea of a barn swallow tattoo for some time. One of my favorite artistic photographs is an image called "Rock Bottom" by

David Hilliard, depicting a son and his father wading in a pristine lake surrounded by lush forest and rolling mountains. The father in the photo has two barn swallow tattoos on either side of his chest, evidence of his time in the Navy, where the bird is symbolic of 10,000 nautical miles traveled. The Sailor Jerry tattoo has represented loyalty, travel, and spirituality to sailors for hundreds of years due to the presence of the barn swallow in unexplainable parts of the ocean and their remarkable ability to always return to their homes regardless of how far they've traveled or how long they've been gone. It was believed that if a sailor died at sea and had the Sailor Jerry tattoo that the barn swallow would carry his soul up to heaven. Sadly, the barn swallow tattoo I wanted was quite detailed and would require several sessions with an artist, which was a luxury I didn't have with only one day remaining in Burlington.

With only a few hours until our appointment, I still didn't know what I was going to get permanently inked onto my skin. The morning was still early and I requested a group pit stop to a local coffee shop so that I could get my caffeine fix. My love for coffee is profound and goes far beyond a caffeine addiction. In graduate school, I took my relationship with java to another level by investing in a home coffee roasting system. Selecting the best organic fair trade green coffee beans, I would labor for hours over my home roaster perfecting the technique to make the perfect batch. After the roast was complete, I would grind the beans fresh every morning and enjoy the brew from my French press, wafting the aroma and sipping each cup to savor the different flavor profiles. While I have since stopped roasting, my appreciation for the process and art of coffee remains an important part of my everyday routine.

In the local Burlington coffee shop, I wrapped my hands around the warm cup of black coffee as I pondered what I would choose for my tattoo. Just then, Aeriel asked, "Why don't you get a tattoo of coffee beans?"

It was so simple, but so perfect. Coffee beans were not only symbolic of my love for the beverage, but more broadly they represented my personal philosophy of valuing the process as much as the outcome. I immediately started researching coffee bean tattoos on my phone and quickly found a design that I liked. A few hours later, the four of us walked out of the tattoo parlor, and on my right ankle was a simple outline of three coffee beans. Not only was I ecstatic with the look of the tattoo, but also proud of what it meant to me.

In many ways, my coffee bean tattoo is a reflection of my pursuit for liberation. Throughout my life I have been socialized to favor the values of instant gratification, convenience, and bottom-line results. However, when I step back to reflect on my most meaningful and significant memories, they involve long journeys that include challenges as well as victories. As a result, I've come to seek out experiences that require me to go outside of my comfort zone, learn, and develop. The process of growing is far more important to me than the end result. It's ultimately one of the main goals I aim for in life.

Focusing on the process as much the outcome can provide a liberating worldview. Instead of worrying about arriving at a certain destination, I've learned to sit back and enjoy the ride. I've become healthier and happier as a result. Instead of feeling anxiety and stress about the possibility of not attaining a certain end goal, I am working toward embracing failure as an integral part of the process in personal growth. Valuing the process has been liberating for me because it allows me to truly accept that I'm not perfect and instead consider how I can improve.

In social justice, the principle of valuing the process as the end goal is crucial to liberation. There is no point at which one will arrive and know all there is to know about establishing equity in the world. Liberation is the process of unlearning all of the biased and discriminatory ideas that we've been socialized to believe throughout our lives. Given that most of us don't start this work until we're older, there are plenty of messages from our families, communities, churches, workplaces, and the media to evaluate and deconstruct. Additionally, those socialized messages continue to come at us, and as a result we must always continue the process of freeing ourselves from the ideas that reinforce and bolster oppressive systems. The ultimate goal then of social justice liberation is committing to this ongoing process of learning and personal growth.

ALLYSHIP

KYLE: Acting as an ally or advocate for any marginalized community requires subscribing to a mindset of liberation. More than a label, being an ally involves action. Actions, more so than individuals, can be in line with the values of allyship. While being an ally can be an identity, it requires reliable behavior that reflects a dedication to analyzing one's own biases and working to unlearn the discriminatory socialized notions that allow for oppression to exist.

Author and scholar Dr. Michael Kimmel has done foundational work around understanding masculinity and how men can be allies in working towards gender equity. His writing and research has been largely influential on my understanding of what it means to be an ally to women as well as to other marginalized groups.

In 2013, I had the distinct honor of working with Dr. Kimmel. During a roundtable discussion with students, he was asked how he reconciles his privilege as a man with being an ally for gender equality and social justice. In other words, the student wanted to understand how one can be an effective ally without co-opting the work or asking those who are marginalized to carry the burden of teaching you about oppression.

Kimmel's response was one that has stuck with me as a defining philosophy of what it means to be a true ally.

He said, "As an ally, you choose to stand with those who are oppressed. They will tell you when and in which direction to walk."

It is not an ally's place to control or direct a movement toward social justice. Because we are the ones with privilege, we are typically blinded to the realities of oppression that members of the marginalized group face. As a result, when allies try to lead in social justice work, they inevitably make decisions that may not be in the best interest of the groups they are trying to serve.

The sole mission of an ally should be to *consistently* stand with the oppressed. This may sound simple, but it can be an extremely difficult choice. Allies make mistakes and are not always congratulated for their work. In fact, there may be times when an ally is being criticized by those who resist social justice as well as by those they are trying to serve. These are the moments when allyship can be most challenging but also most necessary.

If every ally who made a mistake simply gave up and threw in the towel, there would not be allies to speak of. The absence of allies would leave the task of dismantling systems of oppression to those who are marginalized. Allies are important in social work because they are able to effectively engage in difficult conversations around privilege and power with members of dominant groups.

Given that many of us have at least one dominant or privileged identity of some kind, we can all follow Dr. Kimmel's instructions to stand as allies. The challenge is for us to consistently listen and journey in the directions given to us by the marginalized communities we are hoping to serve.

LESSONS FROM A
CAMPFIRE

AERIEL: I love going camping with my dad. Growing up, usually in the summer but sometimes in the dead of winter as well, we'd head out for a weekend in the Minnesota wilderness. My family has a long-standing tradition, going more than 40 years strong, of camping in the coldest of cold conditions. Every February over President's Day weekend, you can be sure that my family members from all around north-central Minnesota are mobilizing, strapping on their cross-country skis and snowshoes, and heading out for a few frigidly cold nights under a blanket of frozen stars.

Whether we were embarking on summer or winter camping, I remember feeling a rush of excitement as my dad and I packed our bags and loaded up the pickup truck with all of our supplies. For me, camping was about spending quality time with my dad in an environment that somehow melted away my nerves and the awkwardness that often surfaced in our relationship. I was four years old when my parents divorced, and I spent most of my childhood with my mom. When I saw my dad, I was often quiet; for me the dynamic between us sometimes feeling stiff with unfamiliarity. Somehow, the noises of nature; the chirping of birds, the rustle of leaves in the trees, and the crackle of the campfire filled the silent tension and set me at ease.

Dad taught me everything I know about building campfires; from collecting kindling, to tenderly blowing on the sparks to help them catch fire, and attentively tending to the flames to ensure they blazed strong into the night. He taught me these skills by showing me. He led by example; never narrating his actions, but rather demonstrating the lesson with deliberateness and care. This is my dad's way. As a true Minnesota man, he is a person of few words. For a long time this troubled me. I didn't feel as though we connected, and sometimes I doubted we were even speaking the same language. Raised as my mother's daughter, I was taught to verbalize my emotions and thus found my dad's reservedness difficult to understand and relate to.

Thankfully, as a young adult immersed in my own social justice journey, I began to realize that there are different, equally valid, ways to communicate not just words, but love. Around this same time is when Kyle came into my life. As Kyle interacted with my dad and me, he offered up a fresh perspective on our relationship. He brought to light subtleties that I had become accustomed to overlooking.

Through Kyle's lens of masculinity, I began to understand my dad as a product of his lived experience (i.e., growing up in a stoic Scandinavian family). This helped me better empathize and appreciate my dad, as well as begin to cultivate the capacity to connect with him across our differing communication styles.

I love my dad fiercely, and I know he loves me too. He may not have been overly verbose about his affection for me growing up, but through the many lessons he taught me—from how to hold a hammer, how to tend a garden, and how to build a campfire— he consistently and diligently demonstrated his love.

This realization and appreciation of my dad has been incredibly liberating. Not only empowering me to move past insecurities rooted in my experience as a child of divorce, but also in my expression of my affection for my father. I no longer doubt his love and as such feel emboldened to express my own. Sure, we may communicate differently, but we have built empathy and compassion that allows us to connect across our differences. For instance, I like to say "I love you," whereas he is more likely to send me text messaged photos of his latest retirement project.

Now that I'm in my thirties and my dad is in his sixties, we don't regularly go camping together anymore. While I deeply miss our time together in the woods, I have continued camping as a family tradition with Kyle. Each time we load up our car with our sleeping bags and food pack, I'm reminded of my relationship with my dad. In the evenings, after we've pitched our tent and we're sitting around the fire, I poke and prod at the flames, sending my dad great love and appreciation.

THE CYCLE

AERIEL: To better understand how social justice journeying can lead to liberation, we must first examine the ways in which we have been subjected to socialization. Socialization is the many ways in which we were taught—overtly or subconsciously—about who we are, how we "should be," and how that relates to greater social stratification. According to Professor Bobbie Harro, "this process is pervasive (coming from all sides and sources), consistent (patterned and predictable), circular (self-supporting), self-perpetuating (intra-dependent) and often invisible (unconscious and unnamed)."

Growing up Asian in a predominantly White neighborhood and with loved ones who were also predominantly White meant that my exposure to other Asians was quite limited. In fact, most of what I understood to be Asian was informed by non-Asian sources. I learned how to be Asian by my White family and images in the media. This learning of my own race, culture, and heritage through the eyes of another informed some of my earliest socializations about my racial identity and led to confusion and discomfort in my own skin.

Early on, I was socialized to believe that Asians were perpetual foreigners—always speaking another language and being from another home country. This was disorienting for me. I didn't have mastery of another language nor did I identify closely with my birth country. Additionally, the stereotype of the model minority, good at math, soft spoken, etc. was pervasive growing up. This became stressful in high school when I felt that mathematical analysis skills didn't come naturally and thus made me question my Asianness. Or when my direct and assertive communication style (informed by my Western/American household and upbringing) caught others off guard which led them to joke about or question my Asianness.

These instances, where my experience was a contradiction to the generalizations and stereotypical expectations others had of me given my perceived race and gender, impacted my sense of self and spurred internalized oppression.

According to the *Cycle of Socialization* model, "We are born into a world with the mechanics of oppression already in place." These systems that benefit some and oppress others are passed on to us without our consent or conscious knowledge. Our understanding of the world and those around us comes from our families—the people we love and trust—as well as from the media, our communities, our places of worship, and our places of education. This socialization comes to shape our expectations for ourselves and others in the world.

As our cultural "brainwashing" continues to mold our view of the world, it is enforced by policies and social mechanisms that reward those who comply with the status quo and punish those who step out of line.

In the end, we are left worse off. This socialization leads to misperceptions, anger, resentment, guilt, hate, self-hate, violence, crime, and poverty for those with and without power. As Dr. Martin Luther King, Jr. said, "Injustice anywhere is a threat to justice everywhere."

The cycle of socialization, according to Harro, leads to the type of world that Dr. King was referring to and inaction is what allows this type of world to thrive. Apathy, ignorance, silence, fear, and compliance with the status quo serves to maintain the systems that allow for privilege, power, discrimination, and oppression to continue.

The cycle of socialization begins before we are even born, as our individual identities are pre-determined. The socialization isn't the ascription of these identities in and of themselves. Rather it's that we are born into cultures, systems, and societies which value to varying degrees specific identity groups (e.g., in a patriarchal society being born male is considered a dominant identity).

Key to moving from socialization to liberation is the understanding of what perpetuates the cycle. For example, fear of repercussion may cause people to keep their heads down and maintain the cycle of socialization. Alternatively, lack of understanding about oppression could lead some unable to recognize or conceptualize how they as individuals might affect change. The complexities of oppression can be overwhelming and can lead to us feeling insecure about how to interrupt instances of bias. Additionally, the fear of saying the wrong thing can be significantly prohibitive to challenging the status quo.

Finally, the cycle of socialization maintains a system of power and inequity. People with power may find it difficult to challenge systems as they have much to risk. Whereas people without power, who are oppressed by the system, may find it difficult to advocate for change in a system that otherwise disregards them.

Despite these very real and sometimes paralyzing restraints to challenging the cycle of socialization, there is still hope. Hope can be found in the process of unlearning what we've been taught. This is what Harro describes as the cycle of liberation.

Generally we are propelled into the cycle of liberation as a result of a critical incident that goes against the things we have been socialized to believe. These critical incidents cause us to question what we've been taught and consider new truths. After some introspection and self-reflection, we begin to realize how limited our perspectives may have been and acknowledge the systems of power, privilege, and discrimination that exist in the world.

In order to better understand these new insights gained on the cycle of liberation, we seek out people and experiences different from our own. We seek further evidence revealed during the critical incident, being exposed to different ideas that will complicate our viewpoints. From there, we begin to build community with others who share in this newfound understanding and organize to create change. This can happen at an individual level or at a systems level, impacting personal relationships or policy and culture.

As we continue along the cycle of liberation, we begin integrating values of justice and peace into our daily lives. We seek out relationships, careers, and lifestyle choices that align with our goals of inclusion and equity. We begin to model these values in everything we do, sharing our vision and encouraging others to complicate their understandings of the world.

Similar to the old adage, "A rising tide lifts all boats," the cycle of liberation serves to benefit everyone, regardless of their social identity. Through self-love, hope, joy, authenticity, honesty, and celebration, both the privileged and those marginalized begin to heal from the destructive nature of socialization.

Choosing the path of liberation allows us to follow the advice of poet Maya Angelou when she said, "Take a day to heal from the lies you've told yourself and the ones that have been told to you."

Indeed, we should take more than a day, and dedicate our lives to healing.

CRITICAL
INCIDENTS

AERIEL: All throughout college I had a number of encounters and incidents that gave me pause and caused me to question, even momentarily, the ways in which I understood myself and my race. I remember one such incident occurred during my senior year. I was having coffee with a mentor of mine. She was reflecting on her professional development and advised me to be mindful of not only how I develop my own professional sense of self, but also to be prepared to navigate how others see me. In particular, my mentor cautioned me about reconciling how others' perceptions about my race may or may not reflect my own professional identity.

Initially I recall being frustrated by this advice. I wanted to believe that I worked in a professional environment which judged an employee for their contributions rather than their race. Additionally, I couldn't comprehend how others could make assumptions about me based on the color of my skin when I didn't fully understand my own racial identity. Granted, I knew that others saw me as phenotypically Asian, but given my transracial adoption I strongly identified with what was characterized as White professional and cultural norms.

The personal and professional dissonance spurred by this coffee conversation with my mentor during college was a significant wake-up call in my own cycle of liberation. For the first time I was confronted by the ways in which my lived experience and early socialization contributed to an internalized oppression that resulted in my desire to disassociate with my racial group. With this new consideration, I didn't immediately move into action, but at least the cycle of socialization had been interrupted.

Shortly after this critical incident I began my graduate studies. This was when I fully became engaged in the cycle of liberation. Through my graduate course work I found an empowered sense of self. My class readings on identity development and systems of inequity facilitated introspection and consciousness raising. For the first time in my life, I had language to describe some of my uncomfortable moments of identity development growing up. I gained the ability to name my experience as a transracial adoptee. I made connections between the various forms of socialization I experienced as a child and the impact they had on my evolving sense of self. Inspired by these epiphanies, I sought out relationships with others who were similarly curious and reflective about issues of identity. This exposed me to communities of racial justice activists who enabled me to make connections between my lived experience and greater narratives of communities of color.

UBUNTU

AERIEL: Ubuntu is a Southern African term that roughly translates to mean "I am, because we are." It became our voyage motto.

In the spring of 2015, Kyle and I served as student life staff on a college study abroad program comprised of 600+ students and 70+ faculty and staff. We journeyed to 12 countries over the course of 112 days. In addition to taking us for the first time to countries in Asia and sub-Saharan Africa, this experience afforded us the opportunity to apply, stretch, and grow our passion for social justice education and our work towards VITAL liberation.

"I'm not sure if you know this or not, but we're sailing around the world on a ship!" was the endearing opening line at every logistical pre-port meeting from our Executive Dean. It became a charming routine for which the whole shipboard community eagerly awaited.

The Dean would push his glasses onto the top of his head and reach underneath the podium, to pull out an inflatable globe and a tiny, squishy ship figurine. In our very first pre-port meeting, the Dean introduced the Ubuntu stick. Apparently inspired by a tradition that had begun years before, the Ubuntu stick was emblematic of the interconnectedness of our community and the values that we held dear. Sadly, somewhere along the fifty years of the program's history, the original Ubuntu stick had been lost. Luckily for all of us on the spring 2015 voyage, our fearless leader took it upon himself to locate a new Ubuntu stick and reintroduce the tradition of bestowing the stick upon a recognized member of our shipboard community before each new port along the itinerary.

Ubuntu is a philosophy that represents interconnectedness. This concept is powerful in talking about community accountability, because it articulates that what happens to one has the potential to affect the whole and that which happens to the whole can have a significant impact on the individual.

The Ubuntu philosophy extends beyond this study abroad experience. With regard to social justice, Ubuntu captures what Rev. Dr. Martin Luther King, Jr. said, "an injustice anywhere is a threat to justice everywhere." The experience of some as targets of microaggressions and marginalization are the responsibility of the whole community to address. Similarly, my own liberation, the awareness and active deconstruction of my own socialized lens, is directly connected to the liberation of my community and peers.

Over the course of our voyage, Kyle and I, along with our colleagues, diligently worked toward fostering libratory conditions for our shipboard community. Early on in the voyage, I created a

Womyn of Color & Allies affinity group. Intended as a brave space for critical transformation, this group provided the necessary conditions for some otherwise marginalized voices to feel heard and empowered. Through various privilege seminars and Kyle's advisement of an emerging White social justice allies group, we cultivated liberation for allies through intentional consciousness-raising.

Elevating critical discourse on the ship facilitated the realization among allies that privilege isn't their fault individually, but rather a systemic problem that needs to be addressed collectively. Recognizing the harm that oppressive systems can have not only on their friends but also themselves, participants realized they can help move allies past guilt and into action. This served as the motivation and catalyst they needed to authentically and continuously engage in social justice work throughout the voyage.

In the context of our social justice journeying, liberation is both a process of critical transformation—unlearning the ways in which we have been socialized to prescribe value and power to some and dismiss or marginalize others—as well as the goal on the horizon toward which we strive as we work to dismantle inequitable and oppressive systems. Liberation is personal and political. In my own social justice journeying, liberation started for me in the classroom.

Through texts, I was introduced to brilliant minds like Paulo Freire and other activist scholars which in turn empowered me with language to comprehend and wrestle with complex concepts like power, privilege, and oppression. What began as intellectual curiosity expanded and seeped into other arenas of my life; I began analyzing interpersonal relationships and taking time for quiet introspection. This process helped me to better form my future hopes and aspirations. What was historical and intellectual grew to become personal. As I deepened my journeying, engaging in critical self-reflection, and moving towards congruence in my personal life and relationships, the personal then became professional. As I centered my study, work, and research on social inequity and strategies for developing inclusive communities, my professional values informed and gave shape to my political beliefs.

VITAL PRACTICE: LIBERATION

Here are some concrete examples of how you can incorporate the fifth tenet of VITAL—Liberation—into your daily life:

- Write out a list of three things you were taught about your different identity categories. For example, write out three things you were taught about your race or ethnicity growing up. Next, list three things you were taught about your gender. Continue with this list until you've covered the D7+ and continue to other identities if you'd like. Seeing the ways in which you were socialized to think about your own identities can be startling and motivating.

- Write out a list of three things you were taught about other identity categories. For example, write out three things you were taught growing up about people who have a different religious belief from yours. Next, list three things you were taught about other genders. Continue with this list until you've covered the D7+ and continue to other identities if you'd like. Seeing the ways in which you were socialized to think about others' identities can be even more startling and motivating. This process will help you begin to see how your worldview about identity was shaped.

- Discuss a critical incident in your life that challenged your perspective with someone you trust. This could be a time where you met someone of a different race or nationality and they weren't what you were expecting. Alternatively, it could be a time when you visited a community and were treated differently than what you had been told. Outlining these critical incidents will allow you to understand the types of experiences that can be catalysts for the cycle of liberation. In doing so, you can begin to appreciate experiences like these that contribute to your own liberation.

CONCLUSION

Action is the antidote to despair.
—Joan Baez

Beginning with core social justice concepts, we explored the various reasons for working toward equity through a common language that can help us get started. Moving into VITAL, we first highlighted the importance of vulnerability in social justice work, including storysharing with courage and learning with humility.

Next we outlined how focusing on identity is critical in working toward social justice. Much of the injustice and oppression that exists in our society revolves around the power and privilege given to some social identity categories and denied to others. The first step in leveling the playing field starts with addressing the inequity related to social identity categories.

In order to engage in vulnerable conversations around identity, social justice journeyers must work toward developing trust. Not only is trust essential between people in dialogue, it is also important for those engaging in the process of social justice. The social justice journey involves many challenges that push us outside of our comfort zones and those moments require us to trust the process, knowing the reward of growth and change is worth the sacrifice.

Authorship is another critical aspect of working toward social justice. When we create spaces where authentic stories can be shared, people are empowered and invested in working across differences. Authorship encourages us to bear witness to the stories that are often not heard, deepening our understanding of the world around us.

Finally, committing to a practice of liberation in social justice work means constantly analyzing our thoughts and behaviors in order to grow. When we lean into discomfort around our mistakes, it allows us to see our insecurities and work toward developing our capacity to create positive change and social justice.

WHAT NOW?

AERIEL: In our partnership as educators, co-founding entrepreneurs, and in our marriage, we live and breathe social justice journeying. By no means is this book a declaration of arrival. We know that a core element to this work is humility and the willingness to always delve deeper and grow further. We have, however, as Malcolm Gladwell describes in his book *Outliers*, put in the "dedicated hours" of intensive reflection and exploration on issues of identity, diversity, and social justice. These hours of journaling, reading, writing, researching, and processing with one another have illuminated for us five core tenets of this work. These tenants—vulnerability, identity exploration, trust in the process, authorship, and liberation—are not the answers to social justice journeying, but rather should be thought of as tools or guide posts along the way.

The co-authoring of this book has been a social justice journey for Kyle and I in and of itself. We have had to learn how to navigate each other's writing and thinking styles. We have spent countless hours together on trains, over breakfast and at the grocery store PANing, learning, and growing in our own understanding of how to practice vulnerability and engage each other's dominant and marginalized identities. We have come to trust the process, knowing that this VITAL message is important, even on mornings when our motivation for writing was waning. We have exchanged experiences of missteps made in the past and collaboratively authored our vision and mission for a social justice-focused marriage and business. As this reflective writing process comes to a close, as we near the end of this book, I am reminded of the importance of action to and for liberation.

VITAL is a framework from which one can craft their worldview, upon which to build one's relationships with others, and towards which one can strive. VITAL is a mindset, a model, a philosophy. We hope it will help you deepen your social justice journey.

The most obvious question one might ask at this point in their social justice journey is, "What next?" This how-to guide has laid a foundation for consistent and effective social justice work and now it's time to take action. Thankfully for us, action means many different things and takes shape in many different ways depending on the person and their individual social justice journey.

When thinking about the daunting list of inequalities that exist in our world, it might be tempting to want to jump up and take immediate action. Logic tells us that big problems call for big solutions, so our instincts might be to rally hundreds of people and start a non-profit organization that can have large-scale global impact. While this is a fine approach to doing social justice work, don't feel bad if you feel called to a more manageable method of creating change.

One of the beautiful things about social justice work is that it's all needed. The small daily actions, like reading a book or having a meaningful conversation with a friend about inclusive language, are just as important as large social movements and political activism. In order to make progress toward equity, change is necessary at all levels. Social justice can be a personal value that surfaces periodically when we feel inspired or it can be a holistic lifestyle that influences our daily lives. Regardless of whether you decide to make social justice your life's work or simply engage at your own pace, your commitment is meaningful and significant.

Social justice is as much about improving ourselves as it is about improving the world. This is why every step taken on a social justice journey, no matter how big or small, is beneficial. Our personal development is the continuous thread that runs throughout this work, regardless of when, where, or how we choose to engage.

With this mindset we can be more intentional about how we choose to engage in social justice. Grappling with our own privileges and insecurities can be extremely difficult, causing us to want to redirect our attention elsewhere. Focusing on action outward in the world can be much easier than looking in the mirror and facing our own imperfections. Remember that the two are interconnected. Personal growth and self-work have the potential to change our relationships, our communities, and the world. Before picking up a protest banner or organizing a group of activists, first take time to reflect on the change that still needs to happen within yourself. Starting there, your broader social justice impact can be more authentic given the personal investment you have made upfront.

Learning about VITAL is not a quick fix or the magic wand to bring about world peace and social equity. VITAL serves as a tool for and toward liberation. You, as the individual, are now empowered to author your own experience, reflect on your own complex intersections of identity, and vulnerably and courageously delve into deeper relationships, conversations, and learning.

How do we ensure that VITAL doesn't just become yet another self-improvement book? To live VITAL means to practice VITAL daily and this takes intentionality and a plan. Like any new skill (e.g., learning a new language) to develop, hone, and maintain your new knowledge, you need to practice regularly. VITAL is the same way. In an effort to define concrete and tangible progress, we encourage you to think about VITAL in 3 phases: today, this week, and this month.

What VITAL action will you take today? How will your VITAL practice deepen your social justice journey? When out for dinner with friends, will you take time to notice the wait staff, what identities they represent, and how those identities may or may not reflect the identities of your circle of friends? Will you PAN (Pay Attention Now) and consider what these similarities or differences may imply? Withholding judgement, will you consider the role of identity and privilege in your social interactions and preferred comfort spaces?

What VITAL action will you take this week? How will your VITAL practice deepen your social justice journey? Will you trust your gut and intervene when you hear something racist, sexist, ableist, or homophobic? When confronted with aspects of your own privilege—which, as a reminder, many of us have—will you stick with it and trust the process, recognizing that the messiness of our own self-work is equally, if not primarily, important to social justice journeying?

What VITAL action will you take this month? How will your VITAL practice deepen your social justice journey? Will you continue challenging the status quo? Rather than accepting things for how they are, will you question the system and cycle of socialization? Will you share the trials and triumphs of your social justice journey with others, honoring that our liberation is integral for the liberation of others and vice versa?

ACTION

AERIEL: Action can look many different ways. As a college student educator and advisor, I have worked with many emerging young activists who at some critical juncture are either so pissed off or so motivated that they feel called to create major change. This often takes the shape of working to start a new NGO or protesting at one's home institution for more inclusive administrative policies. While these are admirable and important forms of social justice action that can most certainly lead to the liberation of oneself and others, these are not the only forms of action that matter. In fact, I have come to believe that how we perceive and define action can be liberating in and of itself.

When I was working at a university in Washington DC in 2010, I co-facilitated an intergroup dialogue on race and racism. Near the end of our seven-week curriculum, we as an intimate group of 14 who had shared lifelines and privilege points, talked about what was to happen next. I recall that one student shared a touching observation that as a graduating senior he had hoped for a capstone experience for his undergraduate career and that our dialogue section—which featured many VITAL

189

principles—became the comprehensive reflection he had been so desiring to have.

Another student shared his experience over a weekend break when he'd traveled home and reconnected with his elder sister. The two had been quite close growing up, but adult life had happened and they had started to drift apart. When visiting together over the weekend, the sister asked what was new at school and the student decided to not only share about classes and co-curriculars, but also about his impactful yet challenging intergroup dialogue experience. This student and his sister proceeded to have hours of conversation about their shared interest in equity issues (the student from an educational approach, the sister from a law and policy perspective). It was through exercising vulnerability and the student's willingness to talk about identity, diversity, and equity with family that served as the catalyst to provide a resurgence and revitalization to this sibling relationship.

I share this anecdote as an example of the many forms action can take. Accepting that social justice journeying and action can be big, small, intimate, or global is important and liberating in one's own journey to go about creating change. It's too easy to become overwhelmed by the self-imposed pressure to "do something big."

This doesn't help anyone or the collective movement towards equity and justice. In fact, this is the final obstacle the cycle of socialization has on our psyches to delay real change and preserve the status quo. If we believe the only action that matters is world-shattering action, we've given ourselves permission not to try. Alternatively, if we can liberate our minds about the many forms of action that are valid, necessary, and effective, we can create a dynamic of empowerment, accountability, and inclusion, which is much more conducive to real change.

SPHERES OF
INFLUENCE

KYLE: As we've seen, the most effective place to focus our energy in working toward social justice is ourselves. Moving outward from there, we can explore our own spheres of influence, which looks like an onion when visualized. In my sphere of influence I am the core of the onion, the place where I can have the greatest impact with my social justice work. The next layer of my onion is my immediate friends and family. This is the group of people that trusts and supports me the most, like my mom, my wife, and my best friends. Think of this layer as the people who would give you the shirt off their back even if they didn't have another one for themselves.

These are the people that will stick with you in a tough conversation about social justice, even if they disagree with you. Because they love you and trust you, they know that your intentions are good even if they might not agree with your opinions. The stakes with our friends and family, however, are much higher than they are with strangers. Because there is love and trust with these people, it can at times feel like these are the most challenging people to initiate difficult dialogue with.

There are times when I go home to visit my family and I am confronted with comments or behaviors that I find offensive. It can be extremely difficult to start conversations around these topics, but don't lose sight of the love and respect you have with the people in this sphere of influence. The trust and willingness to see from a different perspective that can happen when we do engage is exactly the kind of mentality that can lead to positive social change. It is no surprise then that this inner ring of people can be the second most effective place after ourselves to focus our energy and effort in social justice work.

From there the layers of the onion begin to grow larger and farther away from the core. Moving outward from close friends and family we have colleagues and acquaintances, and finally, those people that we have not yet had the chance to meet. While it isn't a waste of time to focus on these layers of the onion, it will likely take more time, energy, and resources to influence the people in these spheres of our lives. Again, change is necessary at all levels. Larger social justice policy and advocacy work exclusively focuses on influencing the outer layers of the onion or those people not in our immediate circles. When we choose to direct our energy on ourselves and those closest to us, however, we have the potential to create a ripple effect that can span across many individuals and communities far beyond our circle of influence.

My immediate circle of close friends and family, or the layer of the onion just beyond myself, is a different layer than my best friend's immediate circle. While we have some people in our spheres that overlap, there are others who we do not have in common. Knowing that I have the potential to impact my best friend means that I also have the potential to reach the people in his immediate sphere of influence through the conversations he will have with those people. Change happens slowly and one step at a time through relationships with those that we know and trust. Beginning with ourselves we can create a wave of social justice that has influence and impact far beyond ourselves.

BE THE TORCH

Though much of social justice work starts and focuses within ourselves, it is important to remember that we are not alone. No social change has ever happened as a result of one person's effort, and it likely never will. While the work we do as individuals is important and crucial to developing a more equitable future, it does not depend on any one of us. Social justice cannot depend on Kyle alone. It cannot depend on Aeriel alone. And it cannot depend on you alone. The goal of social justice will require us all to work together, contributing our unique skills and experiences to bring about the change we are striving for.

This mindset can help us maintain balance and focus throughout our social justice journey.

There will be times when the work we do for social justice is praised and valued. In these moments it is important to remain humble and remember that you did not achieve this progress alone. The positive change that is being appreciated is the result of generations of people working toward a goal that has manifested itself in this brief moment and will continue to develop with the dedication of others toward the same cause in the future.

There will be other times when we are harshly criticized or judged for the efforts we make in this work. Justice can be a difficult thing to swallow and holding others accountable to a higher standard of principles can be uncomfortable. We may experience those who don't appreciate our work or those who will try to convince us that we are too sensitive or too idealistic. In these moments it is important to remain resilient and remember that we are not alone. There are others on the social justice journey who can empathize and support you.

And there will be other times still, when no matter our good intentions or our most valiant advocacy efforts, we fall short. We may be told by those we are trying to help that we are going about it in the wrong way. Or we may become frustrated and demoralized by the snail's pace of social change. In these moments it is important to remain hopeful and remember that we are not alone. While we might make mistakes and we may feel discouraged, larger social change is not dependent on any single action we take. Though many of us may stumble individually, collectively we move forward with every stride we take toward justice.

Our social justice journeys are intrinsically interconnected. We face similar challenges and roadblocks. We can also find refuge, resiliency, and hope in the shared nature of our journey. We believe that you hold, in your hands, a torch that can light the way when you're unsure of where to step next. This torch can also be a signal to others when you need support. Gripping the handle and feeling the warmth of the flame, we hope you will be reminded of our shared journey towards social justice.

As a symbol, this torch reminds us that we are not alone. Rather, we are deeply connected to a community of social justice journeyers that spans history, time, identities, and borders. The flame that you carry was passed on from those who have walked the same path before you and is the flicker of hope for the future. As you continue along your journey, know that you are also helping to light the way for others.

Your journey is well underway. The challenges and roadblocks have been identified. You know in your heart the many reasons for taking the journey, and these have already carried you through many trials in your social justice practice. While your experience and wisdom guide you well, the torch gives you a sense of confidence that you didn't have before. It ensures that your path will be on target with your values and goals for equity. Incorporating the tenets of VITAL into your life will equip you to spark the flame for others, passing on the knowledge and skills you've found to be effective in navigating the winding path of social justice journeying.

With each step you take, we hope that you are filled with gratitude in knowing the process of the journey is growing your spirit and improving your life. We hope that you are compelled to continue because you know the social justice journey is bigger than you. We hope you remember that the actions you take today will build upon a foundation of progress moving towards peace and justice around the world. And we hope you understand that momentum depends on you and others like you to all "do your little bit of good where you are," as Desmond Tutu said, so collectively we can truly change the world for the better.

Acknowledgements

KYLE: First, I would like to thank Aeriel, my best friend and life partner. You believe in me and help me believe in myself. You listen to all of my wild ideas and bring me back down to earth in order to actually make them happen. This book is a perfect example of your patience and love. I choose you. Te voglio, my raviolio.

To my family, especially my parents, thank you for helping to shape me into the man I am today. Your continued support through adventures that carried me far away from home means more to me than I can ever express. Mom, you are my hero. Thank you for everything you sacrificed so that I could see a world full of possibilities.

Before this book was a beautiful mosaic of ideas and stories, it was a bustling noisy street in Delhi, India. Cameron Conaway had the vision and leadership to make this project something that people might actually want to read. More than just an editor, Cameron was our coach, guide, and friend. Thank you for believing in us and in the wild idea that our thoughts might one day make a difference. Onward together.

The creative abilities and expertise of Khushal Chand Khatri transformed the book into an intriguing visual statement. Through different languages and cultures, your design truly captures the heart of our message. Thank you and we wish you many more holidays by the sea.

Finally, to our third set of eyes, Sheenah Freitas. Thank you for combing through and paying attention to the details. We, and our readers, are grateful for your work.

AERIEL: I want to first thank and acknowledge Kyle, my co-author, best friend, and life partner. This book would not be a reality without your drive and vision. Thank you for motivating us to follow through and bring this book to life. Thank you for journeying alongside me, being my torch on our path and adventure together. I love you.

To my parents, thank you for your unwavering support and unconditional love. Thank you for instilling in me a love for stories and a deep compassion for others.

To Omekongo, a graduate school friend, and to Michelle, a middle-school friend. Two inspiring fellow self-published authors. Thanks for your advice along the way.

To our beloved Valentina, thank you for crawling onto our laps and comforting us with your motorboat purr in our moments of writer's block. You are soft like a chinchilla, loyal like a dog, and the best cat anyone could ask for.

In loving memory of Dr. Daniello Balón. A dear friend and mentor who believed in me before I believed in myself. You are missed.

References and Resources

"In their seminal book . . ." Adams, M., Bell, L. A., & Griffin, P. (2007). Teaching for diversity and social justice. New York : Routledge.

"As historian Howard Zinn wrote . . ." Zinn, H. (1994). You can't be neutral on a moving train: A personal history of our times. Boston: Beacon Press.

"Triggers are . . ." Adams, M., Bell, L. A., & Griffin, P. (2007). Teaching for diversity and social justice. New York : Routledge.

"Informed by the work . . ." Brown, B. (2012). Daring greatly: How the courage to be vulnerable transforms the way we live, love, parent, and lead. New York, NY: Gotham Books.

Brown, B. (2007). I thought it was just me (but it isn't): Telling the truth about perfectionism, inadequacy, and power. New York: Gotham Books.

". . . the cycle of socialization . . ." Harro, B. 2000. The cycle of socialization. In Readings for diversity and social justice, ed. M. Adams. New York: Routledge.

Floodlighting Brown, B. (2012). Daring greatly: How the courage to be vulnerable transforms the way we live, love, parent, and lead. New York, NY: Gotham Books.

"In Daring Greatly . . ." Brown, B. (2012). Daring greatly: How the courage to be vulnerable transforms the way we live, love, parent, and lead. New York, NY: Gotham Books.

"The Man Box . . ." Porter, T. (2010, December). A call to men [Video file]. Retrieved from http:/www.ted.com/talks/tony_porter_a_call_to_men

". . . most highly medicated . . ." Cosgrove-Mather, B. (2005, April 21). America the medicated. CBS News. Retrieved from http://www.cbsnews.com/news/america-the-medicated/

". . . creativity and innovation . . ." Brown, B. (2012). Daring greatly: How the courage to be vulnerable transforms the way we live, love, parent, and lead. New York, NY:Gotham Books.

"By 'social identity' we mean..." Turner, J. & Oakes, P. (1986). The significance of the social identity concept for social psychology with reference to individualism, interactionism and social influence. *British Journal of Social Psychology*, 25(3): 237–252.

"Simply spanning the pages..." Zinn, H. (1995). A People's History of the United States. New York: Harper Collins.

"...look back over centuries..." Diamond, J.M. (1999) Guns, germs, and steel: The fates of human societies. New York: Norton.

"We live in a world that assigns power..." Johnson, A.G. (2006). Privilege, power, and difference. Boston, Mass: McGraw-Hill.

"Following the path of scholars like..." Freire, Paulo. (1970). Pedagogy of the oppressed. New York: Herder and Herder.

hooks, b. (1994). Teaching to transgress: Education as the price of freedom. New York:Routledge.

"...women only make up..." Catalyst. Pyramid: Women in S&P 500 Companies. New York: Catalyst, April 3, 2015.

"...we refer to this dynamic as 'salience of identity'..." Callero, Peter L. (1985). Role Identity Salience. Social Psychology Quarterly, 48(3), 203-215.

"...I attended a powerful social justice institute" Social Justice Training Institute. Website: http://sjti.org

"In her brilliant TED Talk..." Hobson, M. (2014, March). Color blind or color brave? [Video file]. Retrieved from https://www.ted.com/talks/mellody_hobson_color_blind_or_color_brave

"Multipartiality is..." Program on Intergroup Relations, University of Michigan.

"In her TED Talk..." Adichie, C.N. (2009, July). The danger of a single story [Video file]. Retrieved from http://www.ted.com/talks/chimamanda_adichie_the_danger_of_a_single_story

"One of my favorite artistic photographs..." Hillard, D. (Photographer). (2008). Rock bottom (photograph). Atlanta, GA: Jackson Fine Art.

"Acting as an ally..." Bishop,A. (1994). Becoming an ally: Breaking the cycle of oppression. Halifax, N.S: Fernwood.

"According to professor Bobbie Harro..." Harro, B. 2000. The cycle of socialization. In Readings for diversity and social justice, ed. M. Adams. New York: Routledge.

"...the process of unlearning what we've been taught..." Harro, B. 2000. The cycle of liberation. In Readings for diversity and social justice, ed. M. Adams. New York:Routledge.

". . . put in the dedicated hours . . ." Gladwell, M. (2008). Outliers: The story of success. New York: Little Brown and Co.

". . . we can explore our own spheres of influence . . ." Adams, M., Bell, L. A., & Griffin, P. (2007). Teaching for diversity and social justice. New York : Routledge.

52165575R00131

Made in the USA
Charleston, SC
06 February 2016